GOTHIC HORROR WORKS

Small Town Crimes

MIKE MORELL

For Paloma

Mike Morell

Contents:

1. Killings in Real Estate.
2. Butchered for Love.
3. Bump the Bastard.
4. Debits and Obits.
5. I'm a Doctor.
6. Mona Lisa.
7. The Rest Stop Murders.

1. KILLINGS IN REAL ESTATE

Peritoneum slashed side to side, I hold in my hands the mass of my bowels spilling out like Jell-O out of a tilting cup. Before I'm gone, my life, now trapped into a small time pill, will flash before my eyes like a movie in fast motion:

"Tac-tac-tac, tac-tac-tac," taps my panicked friend the moth, ensnared in the glass panes of my office window.

My childhood: my parents adopted me at a tender age and called me Ron and gave me their name, Willow. Ron Willow. They treated me like one of their own and made me feel loved and indispensable.

Year 1970: my foster father's employer transferred him from Los Angeles, California, to Delsol, this small border town in Arizona. I grew up like any normal kid would with plenty of nutritious food, a warm bed, school, sports, good grades, and even a car at age sixteen. In high school, I graduated on top of the class.

In the middle of a construction boom, I found employment with Todd Crabbs, my grammar school days' friend. He had a paint business. He taught me the trade. I learnt fast. Like brothers, we loved each other.

We were unknown in the town's social circles, but not for long thanks to Todd. Tanned, trim, his Hollywood looks became topic of female talk in the workplace.

He came to be noticed by Karen Holt, daughter of the largest residential developer in town. Exuberant, her enthusiasm and vitality had peaked at age 37. Big at six feet tall, she wore a full head of red, blown hair, and short skirts that emphasized her popping leg muscles. Always a go-getter, she made the first advance toward Todd to the disappointment of other females around.

Our paint business subcontracted to Max Holt, her millionaire father. We dealt directly with her. She would approve or disapprove all job proposals. We were favored in the bid process. I noticed the difference and told Todd so. Yet, he played indifference, at the beginning.

At the bar, we discussed the matter of Karen. Most people knew she had a crutch on him. I teased him about the matter.

"Not for the world. You see? We're a mismatch," he said.

"She's an overachiever, a go-getter. Could help you out in ways you wouldn't imagine…

"You don't realize what you're missing," I said.

He surprised me over cocktails a couple days later.

"She's just proposed. I've accepted."

"You know the company's gossip? Other girls call her a cradle raider."

"I don't care. You think I'd say no to Max Holt's daughter?"

"You're right. I wouldn't."

"The social event of the year," cackled the newspaper headlines. That Todd had married into money was the street gossip.

In the flower of my youth, I wasn't bad looking either. I met Karen's younger sister Rebecca—Becky—at her sister's wedding and Cupid darted us both with the same arrow. This was true love.

Early twenties, churchgoing, blond, green eyed, sensitive; unlike her angular sister, Becky had a feminine and sculptural figure.

At her urging, I joined her church. She sang at my baptism. I felt fulfilled. My life changed. I turned into Mister Lucky a few months later. I married into money and into beauty as well.

Mr Holt, a kind and generous man, assumed his wife's role when she passed away leaving two motherless lovely girls. With the help of the Church of the Lord, he raised them both with love and understanding.

His role changed after their weddings to lucky Todd and me. In matters of their new marital lives, he kept his distance. For all of us, his wise attitude paid off in the way of familial peace and bliss.

"Becky and Karen never got along. Like oil and water, their characters don't blend. Opposites, physically and mentally. I often have to play the referee," Mr Holt said, and it was an understatement.

Rebellious since an early age, Karen stopped attending church recently in spite of the repeated appeals and prayers of father and younger sister. Her transformation from a devout Disciple of the Lord to a hard drinking party animal happened suddenly and surprised her family. It seemed she wanted to make up for lost time.

One day, things got out of hand. Karen had become pregnant resulting from an unmarried relationship and Becky censured her for not giving up smoking.

When she had a miscarriage, Becky blamed her for the death of the fetus. Out of the clinic, Karen stopped by our house, a glowing cigar in her fingers.

4

"I can't believe my eyes. You're puffing again? Will you ever learn?" Becky chastised her .

"Not inhaling, sis. It's for the taste only. I know what I'm doing and don't plan to quit," Karen said.

"You don't love yourself. You didn't love the baby."

"It's my life. Why don't you mind your own business!"

"You've killed that child!"

"I never wanted it."

"The Devil made you do it."

"No, God's will."

"Blasphemy!"

Becky, in tears, called her a murderess. It looked like the onset of one of those sisterly spats. I had to intervene.

"Hey, stop, will you? Maybe Karen's childbearing years are over and the baby didn't have a chance anyway."

Good choice of words. They disengaged and Karen, sulking, sneaked out to the living room.

Meanwhile, our house paint business boomed. We could hardly handle the orders.

Others would've been satisfied, but we wanted to take a leap forward and take on bigger challenges.

We hung the rollers, sold the business, and went our separate ways. Yet, Todd and I kept our friendship intact.

Real estate and banking were the places to be in a town on the path of vigorous growth. With Karen's encouragement, Todd's career took off. He enrolled in the courses and passed the test for the banking and securities license. He joined the local Delsol Savings & Loan. He handled his father-in-law's juicy financial deals.

Todd's transformation continued. It included a lot more polishing, expensive clothing, learning to play golf. He soon fitted into the pigeonhole of a nouveaux riche.

I've done all right, but more modestly. Following in Todd's footsteps, I earned a real estate license and joined the prestigious Delsol Board of Assetbuilders.

Wake up early, coffee, and peruse the Delsol Herald. Drive to work, answer messages and call clients. Proofread new contracts, troubleshoot complaints—this was my routine, and my family became used to it. Then, drive to the gym, work out and return home.

5

Finally, pre-meal prayer, dinner, retirement early, just like clockwork, five workdays and Saturdays.

We dedicated entire Sundays to God. Dressed up, we arrived at the Church of the Lord for 9am services and spent the rest of the day in and out of Bible school, listening to the preacher's translation of the Sacred Book into the language of us, sinners. Lunch at one, and we returned to school. At sunset, we retired, unwound, and prepared mentally and physically for the coming week's routine.

I didn't allow Becky to work and my pride forbade me from accepting giveaways from her family. It hurt us initially but my income grew steadily, and eventually, her potential income didn't matter.

She proved to be a proverbial housewife, a healer and caretaker of our two girls. We successfully raised model children, God-fearing, honor students, role models for peers and friends.

I had been right all along.

For a while, I struggled to support the family, wife and the kids, then two and three. After three years of apprenticeship, I passed the test and became a broker. I worked for the same firm a few more months. I had an avaricious employer. My colleagues and I did all the work but we received the crumbs that trickled down from his rich table in lieu of pay. Greedy Mr Rose kept the lion's share for himself. Spurred by need, I had a talk with the broker and asked for a decent slice of the commission pie. He turned me down.

"You're over-reaching," he said. "It's expensive to learn. I think you're now overpaid, as I see it."

Providential words! Quitting Rose Realty was a blessing. I established my own office, Willow & Associates. Yet, I opened for business that day weighted down by the fear of failure. To the contrary, business flourished.

Two years later, I bought the office building and my sales force grew to three dozen, largest in town.

Eventually, we grabbed fifty percent of the town's real estate business, and I could feel the envy oozing out of my competitors' ears. I've got to thank the Almighty. Wife, daughters, I, never missed Sunday church services.

I think The One upstairs must have been helping us. Torrents of home listings continued pouring in. Even better, most of them kept selling as fast as they hit the market.

Our clients rewarded us lavishly for our professional and tangible results.

My career took a giant leap when my fellow agents elected me to the local board of Assetbuilders. Ron Willow, President. It filled me with pride.

Things kept falling into place. Because of my business success, management skills and love of law and order, I became Police Commissioner.

Our police department won last year's statewide Excellence Award.

It's been uphill since then, my latest prize, nomination for Citizen of the Year.

Delsol locals behaved like an extended family. Most of us knew each other: the baker, the grocer, the restaurateur, the policeman, the mailman. Many of us had family ties. His wife was related to my wife. His kids were friends with mine and attended the same school, shared classrooms, teachers. Theirs and our homes alternated for slumber parties. We enjoyed such closeness those days.

Then, what went wrong?

July 1, 20xx: idyllic Delsol took a turn south eight months ago. The near-tragedy turned out to be a portent of things to come.

While descending from her car in the parking lot of Holt Developers, her father's company, a masked man hiding behind a van pounced on Karen Crabbs, FKA Karen Holt, from behind and took her hostage.

A secretary happened to peek out the window at the time the knife-wielding attacker pushed Karen into her Mercedes and forced her to drive away. Her eyes followed them out the parking area dashing in a southerly direction. In Mr Holt's absence, she wasted no time calling 911. She reached him minutes later and told him about the incident. He sped back to the office.

From the words of Karen, Mr Holt, and Todd, I put together what had happened.

Following the frantic call from the secretary, police mobilized all its resources. Luckily, Detective Joe Maravilla heard the dispatch while cruising in the area.

His hectic search for Karen's vehicle turned successful as he spotted it northbound toward the Colorado River, Karen driving, kidnapper at her side.

The abductor realized he had been discovered and ordered her to accelerate pushing his knife's sharp edge against her jugular.

"I remembered a defensive course on kidnappings. I knew he would kill me as soon as we reached the outskirts of town. When we approached the Ocean-to-Ocean Bridge, I floored the gas pedal and aimed at a bridge tower. We crashed hard and I lost consciousness," Karen recalled.

Det Maravilla jumped out of his vehicle gun in hand and carefully approached the disabled car. In a split second, the masked man squeezed out of the vehicle, crawled to the edge of the bridge and dived into the river. He disappeared underwater with a splash.

Luckily, except for the scare, Karen suffered no serious injuries, small neck lacerations only. She had no idea who her attacker could have been.

"I noticed something familiar about him. He didn't sound local, but I swear I'd heard his voice before… if it weren't for that cavernous shrill," Karen remembered.

They released her to her family at the hospital. Teary-eyed, Todd and Mr Holt thanked the detective for his fateful intervention.

After an exhaustive and unsuccessful search along the river, investigators speculated the abductor had drowned and his body disappeared down the river's deep, treacherous whirlpools. The explanation didn't lack logic.

Subsequent press reports theorized the body had possibly been recovered but misidentified as one of the many border crossers who drown on their quest to reach the USA from Mexico.

Medical examiners failed to identify many bodies fished out because of the advanced level of decomposition.

I never shared that view. The premonition that the abductor was still alive, stalking us, preparing his next move, gnawed at my entrails. A gut feeing.

The incident triggered the mental woes that have troubled me for the last few months.

The following days, I suffered migraines, nightmares, and dizzy spells. Delsol no longer felt safe for my family, co-workers, and me.

A knife-wielding masked man with murder on his mind confronted my family and me. The chase began. We ran for our lives. Sweat soaked, I screamed awakened by Becky's vigorous shaking. I met her panicked eyes looking down on mine.

"Ron, you're howling horribly, what's the matter honey?" she cried.

"I don't know. Can't explain what's happening lately—a brain tumor?"

The nightmares continued unabated. At hers and our doctor's advice, I rushed to the state capital to meet a renowned specialist. The psychiatrist and his team examined me and ran tests and SCANs.

"We found no brain tumor, nothing wrong," he said. His words reassured me.

He determined the attempt against Karen had triggered an existing metabolic imbalance. I'm not a believer in andropause, though I'm not so sure now. He prescribed hormones, sedatives, and something else.

"Slow down, Mr Willow. You're a workaholic. Take some time off, a long vacation."

"That makes sense!" I told him. "I don't remember taking off from work for over two or three days at a time since my first day in real estate, and that's twelve years!

"The real estate business tolerates no times off. Open contracts lead to open escrows, impossible to transfer or dodge responsibilities. Brokers who take long vacations learn the hard way. Problems arise. Murphy's Law kicks in. If something can go wrong during their absence, it does. Brokers are responsible for their work and their agents'."

A good listener, he nodded. I continued.

"That's how it's all set up. Negligence can land us in court or worse, with a suspended license."

"Don't be shocked with the second part of the treatment," he said, with a smile of confidence.

"I want you to enroll in a martial arts school. It will help you re-establish your ego's balance."

I started training at Tanaka-K&K, for karate and kendo. The sports section of the local paper dedicated half a page to the instructor, Toshiro Tanaka.

The profile underlined his tournament awards and technical abilities, and the tender age he started training. A great instructor by general consensus!

What a character—a fanatic of privacy.

Nobody knew his origins, nothing about his family, except that he was a Japanese national. He relocated to San Francisco for a while before landing in our town. He spoke with an accent.

A loner, he never talked about himself and when asked personal questions, his intensive pupils fired up and his chiseled features steeled. Mind your own business, you could read the words written all over his face.

He practiced the art of taxidermy. When not discussing martial arts, he spoke about it with passion. He dedicated all his spare time to that endeavor. He stored life-size animals in his basement: a deer, a bobcat, a fox, a ferocious brown bear. Apart from his two life interests, he revealed nothing else about himself.

I learnt fast. I never missed a class, seven to eight pm, six days a week, except holidays.

What a difference! The shrink had the answers. My nightmares disappeared altogether. We all returned back to normal. Todd and Karen resumed their previous happy life. They'd forgotten all about the masked attacker. Becky went places and carried herself without fear as if nothing nasty had ever happened. Delsol returned to the safety and quiet of olden days. We loved this nice southern town!

Karen wanted to join us. She said her father and Todd had agreed. A bright business mind, she perceived the potential in real estate. I rushed to hire her. I made sure she notified Mr Holt first.

For a few days, she continued working at her father's construction firm. Meanwhile, I helped her prepare for the test. A month later, she passed and got her state sales license.

September 1, 20xx: she joined our firm as a full Assetbuilder. She learned fast. In a short time, she earned more money than anyone else in the office, including me. Her rich women friends, an army of them, and relatives, hired her for all their real estate needs.

Another human asset, Bill Spice, joined my firm two weeks later.

I knew him from Tanaka-K&K, a holder of a black belt in karate, six-foot tall, trim and muscular. He always wore a distinctive smile on his face.

Prematurely bald, for lack of aesthetic value, he shaved off the hair tufts that clanged tenaciously over his ears. During our training breaks, he used to talk with awe about the collection of knives and swords Tanaka kept in his establishment.

"He's shown me everything, a dozen tanto knives and a katana sword as sharp as a surgeon's scalpel. It belonged to a family ancestor, an ancient samurai. He keeps them in his living quarters, behind the gym," he told me, eyes blazing.

"He's so proud of his martial arts arsenal that he'd exchange and eye for it, if need be. I have weapons of my own. I picked up as many as I could during my Navy months in Japan, but it's nothing compared to his prized collection."

I began a recruiting drive for new agents for my firm, young, ambitious prospects with good connections. Bill fit that notion to a t. He could serve the real estate needs of the numerous military personnel at the base. I made him an offer. His eyes glowed.

"In the service, as a pilot at Delsol Air Station, I met Sandy, a local girl. When I got discharged, I hurried back and proposed. She agreed and we tied the knot two months ago," he said.

"Mr Willow, perfect timing! Sandy's pregnant. Babies are expensive and we need to buy a house. Thank you for your generous offer!"

He started out as my personal assistant and protégé. He learnt quickly and moved to his own office, across from mine. My hunch was right. He became a great asset to the company.

Weekdays, he worked extended hours. Sundays, he opened our offices to take care of walk-ins. His life revolved around family and job.

His ascent rocketed. In two short months, he became a million-dollar producer. The commissions kept pouring in. His exploding income surprised him. Sandy, young, pretty, and exuberant, thanked me whenever she had a chance to.

"It's all his doing. Your husband's very talented," I explained.

October: The receptionist paged my office.

"Det Maravilla's here. He wants to see you."

I fast-stepped to the lobby. We shook hands.

"Detective, glad to see you. What brings you around?"

"Just routine, Mr Commissioner. I hope you don't mind my barging in."

"Course not. I owe my allegiance to the Department."

"Did you know Tanaka-K&K has been burgled?"

"I read about it in the paper, the break-in at Tanaka's. Let's go to my office."

Maravilla explained that the police were interviewing all of Tanaka's students and contacts about the theft. Valuable knives and a rare samurai sword disappeared in the heist.

"Do you have any idea who might have done it?" he asked.

"I can't think of anyone. We all feel great respect for him."

"Mr Tanaka returned to the precinct an hour ago and trashed the receiving room. He caused two thousand dollars worth of damages with his karate kicks. It took five officers to restrain him. He's now in lockup till he calms down."

"He did that?"

"Sure did. And claimed we hadn't done enough to find the $50,000 sword."

"The katana? He priced it very high."

After the brief encounter, Maravilla asked about the housing business. "Superb!" I said.

"Say hello to Becky," he said, and left smiling.

November: trouble in paradise again. I called home.

"I'm putting together the hell of a good deal, commercial property worth a million. Must have the contracts all worked out for next morning's signing. I'll be late, honey," I said.

Becky understood. She was used to it. The receptionist had left since five-thirty pm.

At eight that night, my desk phone rang. I picked it up thinking of Becky, but actually, I was Bill's wife at the other end. Her voice telegraphed frustration and worry.

"Mr Willow, this is Sandy, excuse me for calling this late, but I can't find my husband. Have you seen Bill today?"

"Yes, this afternoon."

"I'm worried. He always calls me when he's going to be late. He didn't show up for lunch today. Not answering his mobile, either. I've called his parents, friends, but nobody's seen him today."

I craned my neck to look out the window. "Wait a minute; his lights are on. Hold it. I'll go check if he's in his office."

His office is across the courtyard, only a few feet away from mine.

I found it open and the lights on. Hmm. Unusual. I returned.

"He's not there. But I wouldn't worry. He could be with clients putting a deal together like I am at this very moment."

I sounded reasonable and managed to calm her down.

12

She hung up hesitantly, more relaxed, but not entirely convinced.

His routine consisted of job, family, gym; job, family, gym. He never harmed anybody, a gentle giant with a child's soul. I didn't give it more thought that night, closed my office and went right home trying to avoid similar situation with wife.

Next morning, Det Maravilla called me up at seven and caught me sipping my first cup of coffee. I liked the guy—a very competent cop. I ardently supported his transfer to Homicide. I'd known him as a uniformed patrolman, and then in the domestic relations division.

"Hello Mr Commissioner, you have any idea where Bill Spice might be? Mrs Spice just reported him missing. He hasn't returned home since yesterday."

"I don't have a clue."

"We think the guy might've gone with friends for a drink and forgotten to tell his wife. It happens all the time. Boys are boys, you know."

"I'm leaving right now for the office. I promise to check around for Bill," I said.

He sounded satisfied with my last words.

I left my coffee unfinished and rushed to my car. My worries started to mount. Bill wouldn't simply disappear for a full day. I decided to examine his office.

It looked the same as the previous night, desk and cabinets packed with files, forms, folders. Like giant confetti, color stickers containing notes lay scattered around. At first glance, it looked like the den of a disorganized person, but in the chaos, I could recognize the office of a busy and successful Assetbuilder. I sat at his large revolving chair and rested my hands on the desk.

My eyes settled on a sheet of yellow legal paper with a name and a phone number scribbled with rapid hand. It didn't mean much. I found other pieces like this, but a computer printout stapled to it commanded my attention. It contained the downloaded listing of a house in the exclusive neighborhood of Rancho Mirage. Under "How to gain access," it read, "Vacant, brokers use key-safe." I grabbed the papers and my master key and locked the office after me. I jumped in my car and taped the listing to the dashboard where I could read it.

Breaking some traffic laws, I drove toward the address printed in front of me.

I approached the gated community of Rancho Mirage. I waved to the guard. He recognized me and waved back. The houses were large and custom made on quarter acre lots, huge for city limits. I rolled down Lazarus Place slowly. I found 1122 and a circular driveway.

How strange, I found Bill's SUV parked outside the entrance. I pulled up behind it, killed the engine, and tiptoed to the front door. I found it ajar, and pushed my way in.

With all the blinds down, the curtains drawn, I had to train my eyes to the dark living room. I flipped the switch and made the fancy candelabra glare like Christmas trees. I panned the room with my eyes. Design was familiar, an open plan, family, dining, and living rooms a huge span under a single vaulted ceiling.

The air conditioner popped on and it startled me. I took a step back. A foul smell insulted my nostrils. Sewer gases backing up? I decided to check out the hall bath.

My knees wobbled... I held myself against the wall... My senses recoiled: Bill inside the circular bathtub, lying in a pool of blood, glass-eyed, fear-frozen. Naked from the waist up, his chest skin had been pulled off leaving the once pink flesh, purple and rotting. In place of his heart, a deep gash exposed the white of the spinal cord.

I touched him. Rigor mortis had set in. The coppery smell of butcher shop became intolerable. I panicked. Some killers return to the scene of the crime! Watching my back, I darted out of the house and dialed 911. I didn't dare call Sandy.

Minutes later, an unmarked car rolled on and stopped in front of me. Det Maravilla bailed out. He called me by my name and entered the house his pistol drawn.

Self-conscious and concerned, he came back out calling for back up on his cellular.

"A crime of passion or hate," he said. "Mr Commissioner, are you okay to give a statement?"

I nodded.

"You've got an idea who might have done this?"

"No idea... He had no enemies."

"You have any information that might be helpful?"

"Not sure, but I'll tell you all I know."

We re-entered the house and sat on the living room couch. Maravilla turned on his pocket recorder.

"You know the victim?"

"Yeah, Bi-Billy Spice, one of my best agents."

"Go ahead sir, start from the beginning. You want some water?"

I nodded. Maravilla retrieved a glass from a cupboard, topped it from a dispenser and put it on the side table. I half emptied the glass. I paused and took a deep breath.

Next morning, The Delsol Herald dedicated several columns to the tragedy: "Yesterday, Bill Spice, an Assetbuilder with Willow & Associates met with foul play. The assailant lay in wait and ambushed him inside a vacant, for-sale house located in a quiet neighborhood. An unknown person or persons interested purportedly in buying the house lured the victim to the trap. The cause of death was not released. The police have no suspects. They have asked the public for help."

A black belt putting up no resistance? I thought. He had to have known his executioner, or, he'd been ambushed.

Delsol went into a panic mood. People prayed for the arrest of the perpetrator. Few could sleep peacefully now. Nothing approaching this had ever happened in Delsol.

Unable to find the culprit, the police released more information. The weapon, a razor-sharp instrument, hadn't been found. Bill, a member of the Good Sam's club, had no enemies. Robbery could not have been the motive. His wallet remained in his pocket and the laptop and briefcase rested undisturbed on the atrium table.

A crowd gathered at his funeral, tumultuous for a town this size. The Who's Who of Delsol showed up. Dozens of colleagues passed by his casket and paid their last respects while his relatives held tear-soaked kerchiefs. I stood near his corpse, downcast. Why do kind men like him have to die? Their productive lives cut short? He left a wife and a newborn.

The pastor recited the eulogy. They lowered him into the pit. I held Sandy by her trembling arm. We threw handfuls of dirt over his coffin just before the cemetery hands covered the casket with shovels of dirt.

Next morning, Maravilla called asking if I would be willing to assist him further in the investigation.

"Delighted to help," I said, and rushed downtown to the Department.

I entered Maravilla's office and pulled a chair.

"This is what we've got so far Mr Commissioner. My team's conducted interviews with anybody that've had any contact with the victim, Bill's close relations and friends. We've widened the investigation to local suspects with violent, criminal records. Have consulted the National Crime Bank, and made local and nationwide appeals to the public. We've set up a task force and telephone lines to receive tips from the public. Still nothing."

"Oh."

"There's only one person we haven't been able to talk to, Toshiro Tanaka. He disappeared the day of his release on his own recognizance after the theft of his sword and his tantrum at the PD."

"His vanishing acts are nothing unusual," I said. "Showing up for training, many times I'd found his place locked up without notice, his whereabouts, a mystery. Then, he popped up couple days later offering no explanation. We're used to that."

"Taxidermy wouldn't be enough by itself to make him a suspect, but the cause of death, the weapon, and the removal of chest skin tilt suspicions against him. And Mr Tanaka's convenient disappearance the day before the murder complicates the issue."

"Tanaka, a suspect? I'm dumbfounded."

"Well, there's no physical evidence connecting him to the crime. Let's say, he's a person of interest."

"Oh."

"It could be a matter of life and death. We must find him."

"Wait a minute. I once heard him say he had a secret hideaway where he retired for practice and spiritual re-nourishment, but he never mentioned the location of his retreat."

"Sir, if you come up with something new, please share it with the department, will you?" Maravilla finished his scribbling and placed notebook in his pocket.

"Course I will, detective."

I found the next Delsol Board of Assetbuilders meeting and breakfast, historically, one of the best attended. It seemed agents found safety in numbers. If Bill had met with foul play—a muscular, martial arts expert—what could someone else, say, a small, fragile woman expect?

16

That was the unasked question written on most faces.

An uncontrolled drone of murmurs left no doubt as to their main concern.

We recited the Oath of Honor as usual and an agent from Realty Brokers gave the eulogy in Bill's memory.

A few sobs punctured the three minutes of silence that followed. I announced the new association policy.

Brokers who failed to implement it would be penalized, fines first and then expulsion from the association.

All new clients had to feed names, addresses, and social security and photo IDs into a central file at the initial contact with an office or agent, no exceptions. While working away from the office, agents had to report their whereabouts every hour, and refrain from meeting unknowns at vacant locations.

The Association would offer a reward of $50,000 for the arrest and conviction of Bill Spice's murderer. The funds would come from the membership fees. In agreement, everybody stood up and applauded. On behalf of the investigation and Det Maravilla, I continued:

"Karen Crabbs' abduction and Bill Spice's murder are wake up calls that have changed the character of our city. This is no longer a safe, nice place for our families and us.

"We can no longer remain helpless against the extreme criminality that threatens to choke us.

"Folks in the Old West were once at the mercy of gunslingers.

"The criminals had a free hand while peaceful people suffered in stride.

"One day, they gathered themselves and fought back. They shot the desperados down or forced them to flee like wounded dogs. They misread the power of people in motion, strength in numbers.

"Like them, we must fight back. Enough's enough!"

A wave of approval unraveled from the audience.

"Keep your eyes open, ears alert, for any news or rumors about the crime, or the whereabouts of Toshiro Tanaka. He disappeared a day before the murder and has not been heard from. Police consider him a person of interest."

Home that night, I thought of my speech. I had to predicate by example, put my money where my mouth was. I couldn't sleep, but then, what was new?

I had a brainstorm. I could become a hero and earn the reward as a bonus.

I decided to preempt Maravilla. While he waited for a search warrant from the judge, I'd take matters into my own hand. I had to find Tanaka's retreat.

I drove to Tanaka's. I came prepared with a crow bar. I twisted out the metal bars of a basement window, got to the glass, and smashed my way in.

I landed in the taxidermy studio, in the middle of a dark hall where chemicals and disinfectants failed to offset the smell of rotten carcasses. In the twilight, I searched for any evidence connecting Tanaka with the crime.

I examined the stock of supplies and appliances: forceps, skinner knives, scalpels; refrigerator, stove, a pressure tanner; paints, chemicals, instruction manuals; a menagerie of animal parts, glass eyes, ears, snouts, paws, huffs, antlers.

I noticed several animals propped over mounting kits: a deer, a bobcat, a wolverine, a wolf, and a black bear. They seemed ready to pounce on me. Their eyes had the breath of life. Tanaka was a genius at this trade!

I froze at the noise of footfall, no, just my heart pounding on my eardrums. I ransacked four chests of drawers. Nothing significant. In the fifth one, I found a notebook. It looked like a diary. I had already spent too much time there. Danger loomed. I stuck the book in my waistband and slipped out through the broken window.

Back at my office safe and unseen, I examined the book. It contained notes, drawings, dates, and a list of items lost in the recent burglary. An address in San Francisco caught my imagination followed by the numbers 1999-2013. The last figure coincided with the year Tanaka opened his school in Delsol. I'd surely touched a chord.

I had to find Tanaka. Contrary to office policy, I didn't notify the secretary of my departure and caught first plane to San Francisco. Soon after landing, I consulted a street map and quickly found the address scripted in Tanaka's notebook.

I leased wheels from Rent-a-Car and rushed to the site. A pet-grooming business now occupied the locale. Nobody there knew Tanaka. I reached the landlord. The previous owner had passed and the property had been sold.

18

I decided to stay one more day. I checked into a seedy downtown hotel, cheap but convenient. From the room directory, I tore off the martial arts schools section from the Yellow Pages. I marked the schools on the city map, then, paid each one a visit.

I had checked the twenty-first when I hit pay dirt, the Nippon Jujitsu Academy on Market St. I showed Tanaka's picture and mentioned his name. The secretary directed me to the gym. I apologized for interrupting the training and showed the instructor the photograph.

"Toshiro, yeah! Where is he now?" the instructor asked, eyes lighting up.

"I've come from Delsol, AZ, one of his students. Problem's he locked the school up and disappeared since beginning of this month, and nobody knows his whereabouts."

"Couldn't help you there. It's been a few years since he taught here. He never called back."

I left empty handed and headed straight for the airport, boarded my plane and returned home. Disappointed by failure, I arrived back in Delsol. I decided against revealing my findings to the police as I had broken the law, and I had run into a dead-end anyway.

People still locked doors and windows. Fear wafted in the air like the odor of decay. After dusk, Delsol turned into a deserted ghost town. With God's blessing, no shocking or nasty incidents unraveled the next two weeks. The town slowly returned to normal.

I saw my career in limbo. Irate clients paraded by my office while I was away. Some of them told my secretary they had demanded the Real Estate Department to jerk my license. My sympathies went with them. I had neglected my job entirely, and someone had to be losing money.

December: I arrived at the Delsol Municipal Course sweat-soaked and short of breath. I forgot about my round of golf with Todd and the important news he had for me. I felt like the one who'd won the lottery but lost the ticket.

I slipped into a fresh T-shirt and changed shoes in the locker room and ran toward the fairway. I found Todd waiting by the first hole. He couldn't disguise a certain disgust at my tardiness. The last years had seen him morph from a happy-go-lucky guy to a no-nonsense business machine, a role demanded by his new position.

Golf was the excuse for this important meeting.

He had nominated me for membership in the board of directors of Delsol S&L, under his chairmanship.

Without speaking a word, I placed the ball on the tee, gripped the iron and gave it a swing. We played the game mechanically, saying hardly anything. He impressed me as quiet and meditative and I noticed a hidden restlessness in his demeanor.

The guy had changed. He didn't mention anything outside the game. I was elated and relieved when we finished the round. We changed shoes at the locker room. On the way out, he finally said something that didn't have to do with golf.

"Ron, I want you to come over to my place. Gotta brief you on board business."

We walked to his BMW. We drove through acres of citrus fields in the direction of Todd's estate, a fifteen-room mansion concealed inside ten acres of orange groves. He had just bought it. I had been there once. We slowed to a crawl and turned into a long private roadway. This winter, fallen ripe oranges littered the grounds and the fruit-loaded foliage evocated Christmas trees.

In view of the house, two unmanned patrol cars blocked the access. The front yard of the house swarmed with police vehicles and lawmen.

Leaving the motor running, Todd abandoned the car. I jumped out and shadowed him. We approached a driverless ambulance waiting by the front entrance with lights flashing and back doors flapped open. He tried to barge in, but two deputies held him by the shirt at the front door. We heard the voice of Det Maravilla.

"He's the husband."

They let him and me in.

"Mr Crabbs," he told Todd, "we wanted to spare you this. Your wife…"

"My wife WHAT?" Todd said, forcing his way in.

"You can see her from here but you can go no further." And he forcibly stopped him in the foyer. "They're processing the crime scene. We'll catch the psycho. He won't get away."

Standing behind my friend, I gazed and my stomach churned. I saw the glossy white walls of the hall smeared and spattered with blood. There was a method to it. The stains were not chaotic. Someone had painted red-on-white abstract murals on walls and ceiling. God, it's so painful to remember!

What came next exceeded even the most gruesome and heart-rending of them all. Karen's body lay not in one place, not even in one piece. She was dismembered like a Barbie Doll victim of the wrath of a wicked child.

The head stood nearest, eyes and mouth wide open. She died in sheer terror. Her once carefully coiffed hair, now disheveled, matted, and sapped in her own hemorrhage. Arms and legs scattered around the hall. The trunk dumped at the far end next to her purse. This one sat upright, sealed, untouched.

Theft was not the motive, but something more sinister and sadistic. An extremely sharp blade did the job. The chops, surgical, clean, and neat through flesh and bone and sinew. The murderer had to be a blood-lusty fiend and expert at dismembering.

Three masked forensic technicians in protective suits gathered evidence leaping and balancing over the blood-soaked floor. I watched with numbed terror, and imagined the house turning, lifting me, and whirling me around in the eye of a tornado. I took a good breath and turned toward my friend. He had collapsed on the floor and two paramedics were administering oxygen.

They took him to the sofa where he lay ashen-faced and desperately gasping for air like a beached fish. They loaded him on a stretcher and carried him away.

I attended a second funeral in four weeks. Like a stake, it went through my heart when the first wound had not yet healed. Karen, my sister-in-law, was so dear to me.

Todd had suffered a stroke and could not attend. Becky and Mr Holt wept like kids who'd had their candy stolen. Other distraught relatives mixed among the throngs. Their tears misted the grounds of Sleeping Lawns after the pastor's invocation.

"She was a kind soul. Never hurt anybody even with her thoughts. The best of sisters and wives. Her kin will miss her now that she's in the Lord's arms for an eternity," he finished, splattering holy water over the casket.

Leaving the cemetery, my sorrow turned to rage. I visualized the butcher punished, tortured, suffering a painful, lingering agony.

I, like many others, visited, and rabidly read the Herald's crime section every single day for new information. I called Maravilla often and insisted he gave me more details. Reluctantly, he gave me some hints about the case.

Forensics returned the report on the fifth day. Stains and blood-spatter did not turn out new clues. Fingerprints belonged to victim and family members. Blood-soaked footprints offered no answers. Attacker walked on cloth-wrapped shoes and wore gloves. The bathtub showed remnants of blood where the perpetrator rinsed himself, but no signs of the murder weapon. DNA did not match anybody known. Killer gained access through an unlatched sliding glass door. The victim was ambushed or she knew her attacker. She put up no resistance, again, as in Bill's case.

I always thought both crimes had a connection. Both victims worked for me. They seemed to know their attacker, a murderer that targeted my company. Who'd be next? We had a possible serial killer in our town that might strike again if we didn't stop him. I began to worry about my family's safety, and my own!

My night woes worsened. Mornings, I woke up sweat soaked and exhausted like a marathon runner at the finish line. Becky's health also deteriorated missing a lot of necessary rest over my night ordeals. Dark patches underlined her eyes. Also unable to sleep, she climbed over my chest and sobbed.

Middle of December: I paid Todd a visit. He had moved to Max Holt's residence and had not returned to work since the ordeal. I rang the bell. The maid answered. I found Todd down on one knee, examining a collage of photos pasted on a yard-square cardboard.

"Hi Todd," I said. He seemed to ignore me. "Todd, how're you feeling?" I insisted.

"What?"

He kept looking at the photos, shots of Karen from her toddler days to her marriage, shots of her last days with Todd. He loved her more than anyone suspected. I decided to end my intromission, turn around and disappear, leaving Todd alone with his thoughts and sorrows.

End of December: My friend Todd Crabbs passed away today. He suffered a series of strokes. Doctors disconnected the life-supporting system at his family's request. He had one chance of recovery in a million. In spite of his youth and good health, Karen's demise overcame him.

The trauma of my dreams sank me into a state of total insomnia. Nightmares returned with a vengeance, so horrifying that my mind adapted with a kind of phobia to the dream state.

Black rings circled my eyes.

My watch said two am. Beside me, Becky had sunk into an uneasy slumber, her closed eyelids twitching, her breathing heavy and laborious, and her parted lips exhaling incoherent words. I didn't dare wake her.

I screamed for fresh air. Had to get out of the house! Work was the only thing that soothed my fractured nerves and I felt a sudden urge to go to the office.

I wore an overcoat over my pajamas and ambled out of the house. I drove to the office, entered, and sat at my desk looking for something to stabilize my fears. A side file cabinet that I seldom used as it kept old transaction files called me with maniacal insistence. I perused the folders.

Every year, I did a cleaning job of the cluttered files and trashed everything older than five years. This was a good time to do it.

I had dumped six outdated folders in the wastebasket when I reached letter J. I pulled a file under the name of Jones. Attila Jones.

It didn't ring a bell, made no sense. A buyer? A seller? I had never heard of him. A total memory block. I unfolded the file and found a key and a lease contract from Security First Storage. Intriguing! I had no recollection of ever setting up this file or having met any Attila Jones.

Hot blood surged threatening to explode out of my temples. I turned off my cellular. I didn't want to talk to anyone till I had solved the riddle of the mysterious file.

I ran to the receptionist's cubicle and went directly to the master files. I checked all sections: under contract, sold, rentals, and every other place in the metal cabinets, but found nothing about Attila Jones. I returned to my office and sat at my desk. I strained my memory so much that sweat pearled my forehead. I pinned my eyes on the key and the rental agreement. I made a decision. I'll check this out right now!

I stormed out of the office, jumped on my car and rushed to the storage. Visibility was poor. I turned on the fog lights. I didn't find anybody around at three am, normal for this hour in a self-service outfit. I couldn't drive straight through, as I didn't have a pass card. I parked outside and rounded the tollgate. I found the grounds semi-illuminated by a few slumbering light poles stooping like morning sots. Shadows seemed longer and darker than usual.

I walked directly to locker #105. Strange, I found my way around as if I'd been here many times before. I grabbed the key, opened a heavy padlock, and peeled the metal doors apart.

A yellow spear from the exterior light pole cut the room in half. I had to accustom my eyes to the penumbra. I found the light switch, but the light bulb had burnt out. Flapping my eyelids, I found a flashlight. I lit it. I fixed the light beam and my eyes on a dartboard hanging from a wall. Attached to it, I saw a portion of human chest skin, nipples and hair intact, and a knife stabbing the centered tattoo of an ANCHOR over the words BORN TO SAIL.

I yanked the knife. I felt it and found it sharp, lusterless, and matted with blood. I panned the light to a poster of Karen's head.

Her face had been smeared with the words CHILD KILLER. I examined the rest of the room. I found empty boxes, trash, bloody clothing and shoes; windbreakers, a sword upright against one corner holding a human heart like a fork holding an apple.

The sword was sharp as a scalpel, shiny like a mirror, and of high quality, no doubt a katana. The stolen katana!

Dizziness overcame me. My knees gave up and I collapsed on a pile of boxes.

I heard pacing. It stopped at the door. My heart pounded like a hammer. I tried to stand up. An old man behind thick glasses, in overalls and a baseball cap stuck his head through the cracked door, his words, a shrill.

"Mr Jones, where have ya been? Ya haven't made any payments since last June, six months, ya hear me? Six months! Yer properties have been confiscated in lieu of rent. It's all legal, ya know. Sorry."

I stumbled to my feet and hid the knife in my overcoat's pocket.

I'm not Jones, I tried to tell him, but he kept his drone.

"Sent ya many letters. Ran notices on the newspaper."

I dashed out the door brushing against the man in my haste. He followed me out.

"Too late now. Ya can't remove nothing. Please surrender yer keys and walk out of the grounds right now or I'll call the authorities."

"I'm not Jones!" my words exploded as I ran to my car, he, in close chase.

I sprang into my car seat but couldn't find the car keys. I thought I'd lost them.

No, I found them on the floorboard. I started it. The man caught up with me and yapped through the car window as I pulled away, tires shrieking.

In my craze, I broke all the traffic laws, sped like a maniac, cut corners. Almost ran over a morning drunk. He screamed obscenities. I watched the rear-view mirror. Nobody had followed me, yet.

I returned to my business, locked the courtyard security gate after me and entered my office. I sat on my executive chair, elbows over the mahogany desk, head resting on my hands. I revisited the storage lease. Attila Jones. I must have an alter ego. The one in my nightmares. A monster lurking in the labyrinths of my subconscious. Attila Jones: blood lusty, homicidal, maniacal, paranoid, schizophrenic.

"Tac-tac-tac, tac-tac-tac," from the window, the trapped moth trying to break out of its prison.

I have a birthmark. A wart on my lower abdomen. It kept me puzzled for years. One day I asked my adoptive mother. She said it could've been caused by an abortion shot. That my natural mother wanted to end my pregnancy, she said, "But you shouldn't judge anybody. God's the only one to judge."

"Tac-tac-tac."

I felt warmth down my right side. Blood had soaked my pants. I remembered the knife I tucked into my pocket back at the storage. The blade had cut through the overcoat and sliced my thigh. I pulled the tanto knife and laid it down in front of me.

Here's my will. And my insurance. I'll place 'em on top of the desk, readily available. I want my loved ones to suffer no penury.

The phone rings! Becky. I pick it up.

"Honey, where have you been? Why did you leave?" she says, alarmed and obfuscated, "Been calling you for hours."

"Ah… ah." Words are hard to come out.

"What's wrong? Are you okay? I'm coming over."

"No! No. Don't. Stay home. Lock up the house. Call police, you might be in great danger."

"Honey…"

"Take care of the kids, and yourself."

I jerk the phone jack off the wall. No more calls. I have to be alone with my demons. The knife will enter through this wart. It will cut it out of my body forever.

Ah, I'll throw the skin away. Messy affair, blood gushing out, staining carpet and clothes.

"Tac-tac-tac."

No more memory blocks... I can see clearly now... January 16, 1970, Los Angeles, California. Age four. Child Protection Services picked me up. Someone reported my parents for child abuse. They found me lice-infested, full of bruises, starved and near death in a filthy room closet. They arrested my mother same day.

I don't remember much about my natural mother, except, she was grossly overweight and told anyone who'd listen:

"I never wanted it. Tried to abort it but he stuck to me. I was only sixteen."

I remember even less of my father. He came home in the middle of the night drunk as a skunk. They argued. He beat my mother and kicked me away when I tried to stop him. She was a bleeder. She stained and splattered the furniture and walls in red after every beating. In spite of her big size, she offered no resistance. Guess she had resigned to her fate.

I remember his balding head, his angry and twisted features engraved on his face like the tattoo on his chest: An ANCHOR balancing over the words BORN TO SAIL. He was proud of it and his service in the Merchant Marine.

Hara kiri. The blade travels like a knife though butter... I see why the samurai favor it... Honorable and clean... Must juggle the blade around... let it work its way through the organs... but leave the heart intact... Ouch! There are some tender parts... stay away from 'em! Let the warm and wormy mass of the intestines spill out through the sliced peritoneum..."

"Tac-tac... "

Outside the office, a sea of lights competing with sunrise. Waves of bright red, blue, and white.

The street swarming with police vehicles and men in uniform armed to the teeth and leaning and aiming at my window. Parapetted behind their vehicles, State Troopers, the blues, the SWAT team. A sea of people, cars, guns, equipment. The News, antenna and van from Chanel-10.

"Mr Commissioner, this is Det Maravilla. Come out with your hands up. You are surrounded. We won't shoot, but come on out," he pleads, through a bullhorn.

26

The night's aglow. Strobe lights, reflectors, searchlights, Fourth of July fireworks ricocheting off their faces.

"Honey, give yourself up. You'll get medical attention. Please!"

Becky through the bullhorn!

"I love you. God loves you. He'll forgive you."

"Ron, I'm Toshiro Tanaka, your instructor. Give yourself up. They won't shoot you. Remember the Code of Conduct."

Yeah. I know perfectly well what a samurai would do.

Can't hold up any more… I better lie down… My body's giving way… It's getting messy… An honorable way to die, beats lethal injection… Feel lethargic… Entering a dark tunnel… Following the fading beam of light… The bullhorn again,

"Honey, you're not a bad person. Give yourself up. I love you."

"We love you. Do it for us. Honey… Honey… Hon… "

Delsol will never be the same. Real estate will never be the same.

Relatives and the Church requested that no autopsy be performed, and authorities complied. My corpse made a quick trip from the coroner to the morgue to the mortician. Along the way, I had my intestines replaced in its cavity and the gaping wound stitched up. My loved ones skipped visitation rites to speed up my burial afraid of the anonymous phone threats.

"He did it without a kaishakunin—a second—to assist him in suicide.

"He died valiantly even if death came slowly by hemorrhage and organ failure and not in the tradition of the samurai, decapitation by the katana's sharp blow."

These words echoed from the mouth of Toshiro Tanaka at the edge of my burial pit.

2. BUTCHERED FOR LOVE

Three hours after Amanda's slaying, Pedro returned home rolling the sedan quietly into the garage. In the chilly winter day, he shivered under his soiled leather jacket affected by a bad episode of the tremors. He entered the kitchen through the side door.

"Everything's so quiet… h-had to be a dream," he stammered.

Suddenly, the fridge broke into an uncontrollable hum launching him into a panic mode.

His heart pounded irregularly, dangerously close to cardiac arrest.

A drone of voices down the hall commanded his attention. He staggered to the threshold and startled his daughters with the appearance of someone out of a train wreck.

Mustache black and wet, cold sweat beads rolling down his livid jowls, mouth agape, he stood speechless.

Myrna, fifteen, held Patty, four, in a tight bear hug, her pupils, two interrogation marks.

"Where's mom?" she asked, knitting her eyebrows.

"Dunno… dunno… out with friends I guess."

"But her car's in the garage."

"Mebbe she… got picked up."

"Patty says she saw her lying on the floor of the garage with blood in her mouth," she snapped.

"Impossible!" he snapped back. "She told me earlier she was going away and wasn't gonna return. I came home… She was gone…"

"Very strange, she always takes her purse with her… Think we should call the police."

"Not gonna bother police! Mebbe her friend, Leona, picked her up."

"If you don't call the police, I will," she said, standing up.

"Okay, okay, I'll call"

He went into the kitchen and found the cellular, dialed, and talked to the dispatcher. "… and she left saying 'I won't come back'," he finished, and hung up.

He turned around facing the master bedroom. Now, fever crept up his temples. Hot and cold stupor. The large bed commanded his attention.

"Amanda, is that you? I'll slip into the covers trying not to bother you," he mumbled.

He arm-wrestled his boots off, collapsed on the bed like a fallen oak, and went into a deep and troubled slumber.

Not for long.

Minutes later, the police knocked. Myrna opened the door.

"I'm Deputy Hall. Did someone report a missing person?"

"Yes, my dad did. My mother's been missing since noon."

"Is there an adult in the house?"

"Yes, I'll wake my dad," she said, disappearing in the hall.

The deputy stood in the middle of the living room scrutinizing the interior. A middle-age man appeared minutes later. He looked gaunt and spent, his thick mustache, scrambled, his hair, sweat-soaked and tousled.

"I'm Pedro Martillo," he declared.

The deputy asked for ID and Pedro showed him his driver's license. The deputy made a note of it.

"Who's the missing person?"

"Wife, Amanda Martillo."

The deputy asked Pedro to give his version of the circumstances of Amanda's departure. "We had little argument 'cause someone was callin' her and she'd erased numbers on her cell phone. Angry, she yelled, 'I won't come back!' and stormed out. That's all I know." Pedro explained.

"What time was that?"

"Around noon."

"Do you have any idea where she might be now?"

"Mebbe with her friend, Leona."

"Do you know where Leona lives?"

"No."

"I know how to get there," volunteered Myrna.

"She's our daughter, Myrna," Pedro said.

"When's the last time you saw your mom?" asked Hall.

"This morning before I left."

"And when did you return?"

"Around three. And when I…" she stops, horrified.

"Go ahead. What did you find?"

"Patty was alone in the house."

"Who's Patty?"

"My sister. She told me she'd seen Mom lying down on the garage floor, blood in her mouth."

"How old is Patty?"

"Four," Pedro volunteered.

"Where is she? Can I talk to her?"

"She's sleeping," Pedro answered pointing to the bedroom. "I don't want her disturbed now."

Noticing eagerness in her eyes, Hall said:

"Go ahead Myrna. What else did you find?"

"I asked Dad about Mom. He said that she'd left in a hurry. I asked about Marisol…"

"Who's Marisol?"

Pedro cut in, "The babysitter."

"Dad told me Marisol'd taken the day off. I told Dad to call police 'cause Mom would never've left without her purse and saying bye."

The deputy asked for the babysitter's whereabouts.

"She lives next door," Myrna said.

Myrna and the deputy proceeded to the next house south of the residence in an attempt to speak with Marisol.

"Marisol's the sister of the lady that lives there," Myrna added.

The deputy encountered a male in his thirties unloading groceries from his car. He refused to identify himself.

"Why, what do you want?" the man asked.

"I'd like to speak with Marisol, or the lady of the house."

"We don't know any Marisol. My wife and I are the only ones living here," the man stated.

The man's wife came out and identified herself. The deputy asked for their version of the events in Mrs Martillo's disappearance.

"Pedro? Yes," the man said. "He came over around twelve-noon to help me with yard work. He had Amanda's cell phone with him and she showed up later to pick it up. They had an argument over it and they both returned to their house. That's all we know. This is none of our business and we don't wanna get involved, period," the man said, while his wife remained silent.

Myrna started crying. The woman took her in her arms, trying to console her. The deputy accompanied Myrna back to her house.

"I was upset 'cause the man was lying," Myrna whimpered. "I think he's protecting Marisol 'cause she's got no legal papers."

Based on the new information, the deputy questioned Pedro again about Amanda's departure. Pedro repeated what he had said before.

The deputy called for a supervisor to come to the scene to evaluate the need for an investigator. Det Maravilla, a plainclothesman, arrived a short time later and got the information that had been obtained.

He asked for a more thorough search of the residence if Pedro would give his permission and Pedro agreed.

The lawmen went through all the rooms in the house and checked every space in which Amanda may have been. They also checked the back yard, which contained a metal shed.

There was a garden hose at the rear of the residence, which went under the gate and appeared to have been used to water the trees.

There appeared to be a puddle of water behind a Ford sedan, however the hose was not close to it.

After they checked the residence, Myrna repeated to the deputy that Amanda might have gone over to Leona, a girlfriend's house.

"I don't know her address or phone but I do know how to get there," she added.

Pedro gave his permission and Myrna accompanied Hall in his attempt to locate Amanda.

Meanwhile the other detective decided to try to contact Amanda's family members in an attempt to locate her.

Myrna directed Deputy Hall to 666 Tombstone Drive to try to find Amanda or her friend, Leona. The residents appeared to be all farmhands. There were five males and three females present. The deputy obtained identification from the female residents, neither of which was Amanda or Leona.

An Attempt To Locate on Amanda Martillo was issued and the subject's information was entered into the NCIC.

Working without an entry visa, Pedro accepted a job universally avoided, even by other migrant workers like him, dusting farm fields with insecticides from a pickup truck.

Like other dusters, migraines and allergies pestered him. However, he kept on. He was built like someone out of Muscle Beach and the pay was good—transferred to pesos. In addition, he and his friends were putting cheap vegetables on American tables—something to be proud of.

She was young, he, twice her age.

Love and convenience were the issues.

Marriage would definitely help him with his resident visa and work permit, enhance his career opportunities, and make him eligible for promotions and salary rises.

Eighteen, Amanda, pretty, petite, father-less since an early age. She was homesick and likely prey for on-the-job harassment. Pedro seemed to have been god-sent. They decided to move in together and raise a family.

Like millions of other farmhands, Pedro and Amanda worked year-round, summers in Selina, California, winters in Delsol. Their combined income pushed them up to the middle class bracket. They were realizing the American dream.

Two daughters were born: Myrna and Patty. This family lacked closed friends. They were not exactly social outcasts, but the continuous moving and the consequent changes of dwellings and work locales rendered long-lasting relationships shaky and short-lived. Most of their acquaintances were of the cursory type.

Amanda had a sister. She had married into relative wealth and rarely called or said hello maybe for fear of being contaminated by the less affluent. Recently, Amanda had become orphan of mother.

The elderly woman had been in agricultural labor most of her life and had just died of a brain tumor after months of irrational behavior.

Many of her co-workers had died of brain tumors.

All of Pedro's family lived abroad and had become estranged. They no longer cared to call or write.

This family stuck together and relied on each other more than usual. Contrary to norm, Myrna did not see Patty as a threat in the peer hierarchy, but as a child of her own. She took care of her, fed her, protected her, and tried to play the surrogate mother.

Likewise between spouses. For years, they treated each other with love and respect.

The Martillos agreed to buy a house in Delsol.

On their eleventh anniversary, they qualified for a loan on a new house, nothing luxurious but a good-size three-bedroom-frame-and-stucco in a working-class neighborhood.

Pedro and Amanda concurred with the house and the location.

High block fences surrounded the house. It was independent and protected from the hot desert sun by the neighbor's large shade trees.

The construction was completed within two months and the family moved in by the end of the work season. Before leaving back for Selina, they asked the next-door neighbors to keep an eye on the house. For the first time they had made friends of a permanent nature. Pulling away from the carport, the departing family waved "So long!" from the moving van.

However, six weeks ago, dark clouds were looming over this family's horizon and their idyllic American dream.

Myrna, having been accepted into the school cheerleaders' team, hung her newly starched black and white uniform and pom-poms outside her room's closet before leaving for school.

Pedro, ambling around the house opened her room's door. The sight of the uniform shocked him like a bolt of electricity. Like possessed, he yanked the uniform from Myrna's room, hurried to the back yard, and burned it to cinders in the BBQ broiler.

All the members of his family confronted him that night. He made them sit around the dining table and started to preach:

"The uniform had the colors of the pirates' flag. I had to take action and protect you, my family, from the menace of corsairs lurking around. You must understand."

Family members acted as if his words were logical, and carried on as usual. At his insistence, Myrna dropped out of the school team after a tearful episode of rebellion.

The next Monday Pedro stayed home, missed work. He felt upset, couldn't explain it, a general malaise. He thought of Amanda.

She was away working. His suspicions bubbled.

Home's the place for decent women. She otta quit workin'; stay home like a good homemaker. Instead, she won't listen. She ignores me.

A few days later, he shocked his family again.

He had shaved his head. Initially, they laughed heartily at his appearance but soon stopped the giggles when he told them it was no joke; he meant dead-serious business.

"Afraid beetles were nesting on my scalp. I had to get rid of 'em," was his explanation.

They had continuous arguments. Myrna was becoming a woman, but in Pedro's eyes, she didn't cease to be a child. He wanted her raised the old-fashioned way: few amusements, home every night, lots of house chores.

Rebellious, she argues all the time 'cause she knows her mom's on her side, he thought.

Fifty-something, tired, falling apart, penile dysfunction wrecking self-esteem, his mind worsened:

Angel or devil? Shall I ignore the gossip? I must catch her in the act. Find out what she does behind my back.

The next few days Pedro saw his relationship with Amanda taking a nosedive.

He couldn't watch her on the job because she'd been assigned to another ranch. Still he overheard a worker saying "Fabulous ass and tits." He couldn't be referring to any other than Amanda, he thought, convinced now of her duplicity.

Can feel their laughs behind my back. Now, she's turned the girls against me. They despise me. "Cabrona!" he repeated, obsessed.

Migraines and nightmares worsened. He lost more weight, avoided sex, raised his voice without provocation, often snapped at her daughters. He slapped Amanda for the first time, then, he felt revolted and begged for forgiveness. Things quieted down for a while, but the abuse continued. Pent-up anger followed by tearful episodes of repentance. Typical rollercoaster.

Christmas, a day of joy, but not at the Martillo's.

Amanda found him home. He'd missed work.

"Pedro, are you okay?"

He nodded and smiled. She could not get a word out of him. She phoned his supervisor and this one told her he'd had no choice:

"Think he's working too hard. Had to let him go. Don't worry. Ain't gonna fire him. Under a lot of stress. Just needs some rest, time off."

Mouth agape, she pressed the headpiece against her ear.

The super added: "Was ordering lettuce pickers to wash and sterilize the harvest knives or throw away the whole crop. Management couldn't put up with that. When I discovered this morning he'd ordered fifty gallons of industrial alcohol to disinfect the knives, I had to let him go."

That day, December 25, coming back from the neighbor's house, Pedro confronted Amanda in the kitchen regarding the calls on her cell phone. She raised her voice:

"I'm sick of your crazy bullshit. Leave me alone!"

She lifted her hand to slap him. He dived for her neck. She dropped the cell phone and clutched Pedro's hairy arms. Her nails punctured his skin and drew out some crimson fluid. She was no match. His powerful hands went through bone and sinew like a nutcracker.

Squeezed… Squeezed… Squeezed… One minute, two, three, an eternity. "Punishment's not enough for the evil entwined in her heart," his alter ego bullied him. "She's done you so much wrong!"

He squeezed harder... harder.

"She'll laugh behind your back no more."

Squeezed...

Mouth still, silent, lips parted, neck folded like a broken doll's, blood dripping out of her mouth and ears and urine down her legs, she collapsed in his arms.

He laid her down on the kitchen floor. His head, a torch, his breathing, heavy and laborious, he wiped with his shirt the white nose discharge and foamy mouth spittle. He dragged her out through the kitchen door. In the two-car garage, the other vehicle was the van, his car.

He laid her down by Amanda's sedan, unlocked the door, and switched the trunk door open. Her mouth bled more profusely and he went to retrieve garbage bags from the kitchen.

Little Patty, who had awakened, appeared at the hall carrying a Barbie doll. She walked into the kitchen. The top part of Mom's body was visible behind the door. She ran up for a better look. Pedro slammed the door in front of her.

"Your mommy was drunk and went to sleep, she's gonna be all right. Go back to your bedroom now," he ordered.

"She went beddy bye? I'm going beddy bye too," she said running away with little steps and little child's giggles.

Pedro checked the floor of the kitchen where the incident had happened and noticed blood droplets over the white ceramic tiles. He ran out through the sliding glass door to the patio and grabbed a mop and a bucket. He filled up the bucket with water and poured in a cup of bleach, then, re-entered the kitchen and mopped off the red impact stains.

He poured the water that had turned pinkish into the hall toilet and flushed it down, grabbed the garbage bags and returned to the garage.

Waiting motionless, Amanda was still there, same place he had dropped her.

"You're peaceful, innocent, angel-like."

Bleeding had stopped and her lovely tan changed to paper white. Rigor mortis and the pangs of remorse were setting in, but there was work to do.

He put the bag over her face, slid it over her torso, lifted her, and pushed her in the trunk.

Stammering around the garage, he picked up a shovel and placed it beside the body. In a genteel gesture, he closed the door slowly.

"Amanda, I did it for love, remember that," he whimpered, over the closed trunk door.

He went back out, opened the faucet, and pulled the garden hose into the garage. He hosed off the area where Amanda had lain, returned the hose, shut off the water, jumped briskly into the car and started it.

He was full of a determination he hadn't experienced for a long time. With the remote, he opened the garage door and drove away in a southerly direction.

Calmed down in spite of high fever, he drove mechanically through seldom-used service roads except during harvesting. He labored instinctively, as if acting from a script—a crime show he saw somewhere on television.

He reached one of the farthest ranches where his employer reaped lettuce. The planting season was over; the land was dry and idled, and crickets and rodents had moved to greener fields. A stench of rotten flesh—dead wild animals—slapped his nostrils. Vultures scattered at his approach.

He was in land leased by his agro-business every annual season. There was an easement on one side, an abandoned three-foot deep canal scheduled to be refilled, leveled and added to the cropland shortly. It was strewn with dead branches, leaves, and venomous crawlers.

He alighted and scanned the area, then picked a point where he knew the canal was deeper. He went to retrieve the shovel from the car's trunk and returned to dig a niche through the sand and debris.

Short of breath, he went back for the body, laid it down, and replaced the dirt and debris. Back by the car, he threw the shovel in and slammed the trunk.

"Gotta head back home."

A draft of wind raised a dust storm. The chaparral seemed to advance and encircle him. He heard laughter and held his breath. The wind subsided and the fields returned to stillness and silence.

"Nobody's seen me," he said, more relaxed.

Switching on, he prepared to steer away but gazing back at the grave noticed an arm and a leg sticking up over the debris.

The hand cramped up to the sky like clamoring for vengeance. Rigor mortis had stiffened her limbs in grotesque shapes, but he suspected otherwise.

"Pendejo!" he exclaimed, blaming himself for his carelessness, "could she be...?"

He got off and approached with caution. He touched her hand and felt her wrist.

"She's frozen cold!"

Yet, the stiff-as-wood arm and leg would not bow down. He returned to the car, re-opened the trunk and retrieved a razor-sharp harvesting knife. In able hands, the knife cut easily by the elbow and knee through flesh and sinew.

He re-interred the severed limbs, returned to the car and drove off escaping through the dust devils attempting to encircle him.

Six weeks later a canal crew, attracted by a foul smell and a crowd of vultures, found a bleached skull and bones and tattered clothing. Tooth and DNA identification matched the remains to Amanda Martillo.

"The cause of death is strangulation," declared the medical examiner.

An APB was put out for the arrest of Pedro Martillo, but he had skipped town. He had told neighbors he was going to hop the trains. Hard to find anybody in the railroads. Like a needle in a haystack.

However, a few weeks later, bailing out of a railroad car carrying swine an over-excited hobo declared to the railroad police: "Complained of voices inside his head, migraines... Pulled a piece from his waistband and the sonuvabitch blew the top of his head off... Panic-stricken, we scattered!"

They found the gun and Pedro's headless body. The pigs had eaten away at his wound. The PD closed the case.

3. BUMP THE BASTARD!

Delsol, Arizona, is no Garden of Eden by any measure. It suffers its share under the crime burden. Petty theft, graffiti, and gang activity are on the upswing to the dismay of the well-established, law-abiding citizenry.

Murder of the vilest kind is the exception rather than the rule, but what can be called what happened that winter evening of 20xx?

The news of the slaying of a rich, well-liked local farmer—so enamored with food and drink and the joie de vivre—the previous night, outside a well-known restaurant, where he and his wife had just had dinner, shocked the town to its foundations.

The senseless, seemingly random act of violence threw the population into fear spirals. Delsol, the destination of many running away from big city crime, had occasionally witnessed murder, but never where there seemed to be no motive, and the victim had been so highly regarded. His death at the hands of another in such a despicable way was a travesty and something that should never have happened.

I'm Lt Maravilla.

From my long experience with crime, evidence from facts and witnesses and my notes, I'm confident the following is what really happened or at the least, the most likely scenario:

That night Jeremy Burns gorged on, purportedly, the best burgers west of Chicago: hearty full-pound meals prepared with house-ground sirloin and Cheddar cheese stacked on house-baked buns; topped with house-made mustard and sauces and with generous sides of house fries.

Mr Burns' healthy appetite measured up to his 50-inch girth. He consumed several burgers and washed them down with several quarts of ale.

While his wife, Bonita, ordered a tossed salad and left most of it untouched on the plate, Jeremy finished his food, drank up the last of the brew and prepared to pay the bill. On the way out, he tipped handsomely the waiter before placing his Stetson hat over his shaved head. He said "Bye" through his toothpick, and the owner of Texas Eats obliged with a friendly "Good bye folks, come back soon."

He wrapped one arm around nude, ivory-skinned Bonita's shoulders and stumbled out the back exit to the parking lot. Out the door, neither he nor Bonita noticed the strange exception the normally dry, clear desert had in store for them. Ominous fog had turned the night pitch black while a dust devil sneaked up and slammed square into the couple and stung their faces.

Standing by his dual-ton GMC pickup, rifling for the keys in his pocket, he felt a call from Nature. Unzipping his fly he discharged while Bonita hopped aside to avoid the abundant and foamy torrent spread out by the wind. Patiently and silently, she waited.

When finished, he shook it off repeatedly, replaced it in the cave of his shorts, and wiped the wet off his hands with the side of his pants. He opened the truck door and rolled in. Once on his seat, he remembered about the missus and unlocked the passenger door.

"Jeremy, love, you're horribly drunk. You sure you can drive? Remember Jimbo. He just got out of jail for DUI."

"Shut up woman, hic! Beer don't affect me like it does my dumb brother, hic! Course I can drive," he said loosening his collar. "It's hot in here." Puffing, he reached for the button, rolled down the windows and felt for the ignition keyhole.

What happened next shocked Bonita to the bones. "I couldn't believe. It looked like a pipedream," she declared later between sobs.

Getting ready to slide into her seat, she heard a pop and another a second later. Jeremy had been shot in the temple twice at close range while trying to switch on the engine.

His toothpick shot out of his mouth like a projectile, and he slumped over. The freefall of his head cracked the steering wheel. His wounds let the blood out like open spigots flooding the cabin's leather interior.

She looked in horror and jumped out the window, as in the fight or flight instinct, then ran back to the restaurant and called for help.

Minutes later, she declared to the first lawman on the scene, "Couldn't do anything to prevent it... It was so sudden... Terrified and afraid for my life... He spared me, thank God."

She rushed to the hospital for a routine checkup where she was administered sedatives. Hours later, I, Det Joe Maravilla of Homicide, met her at the Burns ranch and took down her declaration.

"Mrs Burns, there are no witnesses. Nobody's heard anything. We've found the gun and have put a trace on it. Please tell me what happened to the best of your recollections."

"As I told the officer..."

"Please repeat it again," I said retrieving my notebook.

"Sitting in the passenger seat, I saw the face of a man on the driver's window. He raised a gun and shot my husband and disappeared. I froze. Then, I jumped out and ran to the restaurant."

"Did you recognize the assailant?"

"No one I knew. Couldn't take a good look at him. Dark hair, maybe Spanish. I was so scared."

She sobbed swabbing her nose with a Kleenex.

"All we have now is mangled bullet fragments and the powder residue on the driver's side. The test for gunpowder you volunteered to was negative as we expected."

"I'm happy to be of any help."

"You have an idea who might've wanted your husband dead?"

"I refuse to believe it, but there's someone who'd benefit greatly, his daughter Rosemarie Burns. She's the sole heir. In her deathbed, the first Mrs Burns left everything to her and Jeremy abided by her last wish. I never contested it. It was natural to bequest everything to a biological offspring."

My next logical step was to interview Rosemarie. She came to my office accompanied by her boyfriend. Twenty-one, she wore extreme make up and a ring in her nose.

"Bonita did it," she said before I could ask my first question. "I warned my father about her. She never loved him. All she wanted was to get at his money and she got plenty of it. She's always been a shopaholic and spendthrift."

I took down her declaration with a grain of salt. I remembered a day years back before the passing of the first Mrs Burns. I'd been summoned to the Burns' ranch because of a domestic disturbance. Rosemarie and her boyfriend, Jerry Howitzer, a well-known local punk and junkie, had been asked to move out of the house.

The pushing and shoving turned physical and Rosemarie had slapped Bonita. Mr Burns came to the aid of his wife and called police.

The young couple agreed to leave that night and remove their belongings later; but as they walked out the door, they made death threats against the Burns.

Rosemarie had been in trouble with the law. Still on parole, she'd served time for theft and drug use. Rather than a reliable witness, she looked more like a suspect.

As to Bonita, everybody had her in high esteem. Elegantly conservative in dress, active in private charities and, with her husband, a regular attendant to St Paul's Catholic Church, she appeared to be a most unlikely murderess in spite of Rosemarie's suspicions.

"We've interrogated and checked the alibis of all the employees at your husband's ranch and the Texas Eats restaurant." I paused as she sobbed, "I'm sorry Mrs Burns. My sympathies are with you…

"We'll catch the culprit, I assure you." I waited till she calmed down, "We've contacted everybody with connections with your husband. I'm sure the Herald's offer of the $10,000 reward will turn up some leads. Somebody out there knows something. The composite of the suspect you dictated to the police artist's been distributed to lawmen in several jurisdictions."

For hours, I've interrogated Rosemarie and her boyfriend. I couldn't find anything to tie them to the murder. Their alibi was they were together shooting drugs when the crime took place; however, I told them they were persons of interest and better to remain in town in case they were called back.

The investigation lost steam.

The small town police department had its share of new crimes to solve, and only I remained on the case after two months of fruitless efforts. The dossier had to take second place to other cases.

I mulled over the motive. Racially motivated? After all, the victim was Anglo and the killer thought to be Spanish. Or perhaps an act of vengeance from a fired or disgruntled ranch hand? Or maybe no motive at all, just a random killing, the most difficult to solve?

"Jeremy had no enemies," one of his drinking pals told me. "What a guy! He donated heavily to St Paul and was a great tipper. Waitresses adored him. He never failed to leave a twenty on the table. While his wife was out of town, he'd take me and the rest of the gang to the Paradiso. He always insisted on paying the bill.

"He loved to sit at the edge of the catwalk and have the dancers slap him across the face with their naked boobs. Waiters lined up pitchers of beer in front of him while he tossed away hundreds and twenties like a Santa Claus gone wild. Beats me to think someone wanted him dead."

The fifty-car motorcade rolled along Main Avenue. Bonita rode in the first car behind the black hearse. The car procession disbanded when it reached Sleeping Lawns and people congregated inside the mortuary. Jeremy looked radiant in the tuxedo, plumed chapeau, cape, and ceremonial sword of the order of the Knights of Columbus. The cemetery hands carefully lowered the casket into the pit. Reverend Perry gave the invocation.

"When he was taken out, a full, loving, beautiful light was extinguished leaving us in darkness. But who would do it in such a violent way? The answer lies in the hands of the police…

"But whatever the outcome, the main premise remains, no one could've had more friends."

Yes's peeled off from the attendants.

As Bonita stood at the edge of the pit, her eyes pierced Rosemarie and her boyfriend Jerry like harpoons for signs of joy or culpability but nothing telegraphed through the wide dark glasses worn by the pair. And they returned the stare.

"He had a full life on earth, and now we can rejoice that he's reached the fullness of life in heaven. He feasted at the earthly banquet, and now feasts forever at the heavenly banquet. He is now with God, and like Him, is in all places, at all times forever," Perry continued, sprinkling the grave with holly water.

The fight over Jeremy's assets was nasty to the last penny. Bonita sued over the assets and received a cash stipend. After three months of wrangling, Bonita accepted an undisclosed cash settlement.

* * *

Six moths prior to Jeremy's violent adieu, Bonita had won the food and beverage concession at the Castle Inn, the best and newest hotel in town. The hotel needed a new caretaker for its Crystal Room—a sumptuous restaurant and bar—and Bonita was the obvious choice due to her restaurant experience and knowledge of haute cuisine.

Her dreams had crystallized.

For the first time, she'd become owner and administrator of an eatery, and not merely a salaried hand.

After she'd spent most of the funds provided by Jeremy stocking and redecorating the restaurant-bar, the end result filled her with pride. Inauguration day, most of Delsol's Who's Who showed up. She prepared a lavish buffet to the delight of the guests, especially Jeremy and his gluttonous friends.

Things did not turn out as expected. The stream of diners fizzled out to a trickle the following days. Income plummeted. The diner had become a money-gorging hog. The Crystal Room's opening was premature and not ready for big times yet. Week after week, it operated in the red.

A few nights before Jeremy's death, Bonita looked pathetic: emaciated, tired, spent. Unknown to her, all previous food concessions had failed at this location.

Tourism was not a big deal in Delsol those days just yet. Few locals patronized the luxury diner, or leased it for private parties. Bonita had spent sleepless nights reflecting on the reasons for the failure. The bar remained mostly empty. Her savings plummeted precipitously. She was sinking deep into debt.

Those days, Bonita outdid herself to keep the diner from collapse but expenses eventually caught up with her. The kitchen help had just deserted her after she failed to hand them their paychecks for still another week. They no longer believed in her words, or in miracles.

In a last desperate attempt, she tried to run it as a one-person operation doubling as cook, waitress, dishwasher. Her appearance suffered. Her grease-stained face, uncoiffed hair, and stained clothes belied her advertised image of a successful restauranteur.

Back at home, in the master bedroom, she demanded more money from Jeremy:

"You're a rich bastard. I know you've got millions stashed up somewhere! The more they whimper, the more they have, so it goes."

"I'm not spending another penny on that stupid idea! You've got no nose for business. Stop wasting money. It's time to quit and stay home where you belong."

"You're crazy if you think you married a maid."

"You belong cookin', cleanin', doin' laundry. That's the only thing you're good for."

"The hell if I'll do that." But she'd talked into dead ears. He'd turned away in bed and dozed off.

"No use talking to a sleeping, snoring mountain!" she screamed.

The diner's situation deteriorated. The butcher, the grocer, the landlord could not wait any longer. They stopped deliveries and eviction was imminent. Bonita was desperate and angry the night Mario Ricardo came into the screen.

A godsend, he's what I need, she thought when she sat at the split level bar next to him. Dressed in polo shirts and well-pressed slacks, debonair, svelte, sociable, with a full head of wavy dark hair with elegant side touches of grey.

It didn't escape Bonita that he'd hung around the Castle Inn's bar for a few nights, dancing and romancing an occasional elderly lady to the beat of the piano bar and the wails of the balladeer.

43

Or chatting with other patrons, or the bargirls.

"Invited by an old friend from Galveston, I recently landed in town," he told her, during the introduction.

I know his type, a small-time hood without visible means of support launched to hunt for rich old women in trendy bars. He doesn't fool me... I'll go along with his charade anyway, she thought.

"I'm in the thoroughbred business, but my Arabians've had bad luck at the track lately," he added.

See? I told you.

Gin Collins was his trademark but the bargirl asked him anyway.

"Yes, always the same," he said, inviting Bonita to have a drink with him.

A gigolo, cunningly he hides under chitchat his real intentions. I've sized him up and will use him to my best advantage.

She ordered a martini. She noticed he pulled his last bill from his wallet. He handed a twenty to the bargirl and told her to keep the change.

During the first meeting—the first round of social boxing—they had a long talk.

Sex was part of her strategy. The next evening, the check for the libations paid by the house, drunk and leaning on each other, they sneaked to her private suite.

The suite was included in her hotel package and she was still able to use it at her convenience.

Next day, they returned to her suite for an encore. Ricardo lay on his side of the bed. Bonita, unscathed in her robe after a shower, sat on his side sharpening with the file her nails.

"What, dead or just sleepy?" she asked.

"Dog-tired."

"Told you. Men are no match for women."

"Younger, no woman could outlast me."

"Oh yeah, and a big liar too."

"What time is it?"

"Eight."

"Eight only! Please, I need some rest."

Bonita's single mother worked hard at various menial jobs to give her only daughter a good education.

She wanted Bonita to imitate the life of the Rich and Famous even if the backing funds were lacking.

She managed to send her to a social etiquette academy and succeeded in grooming her as a socialite even if only skin deep. Bonita learned to walk like a model on a catwalk, and talk with distinction. Pretty and slender, she managed to fool many people.

Different story now, she didn't mind showing her real self to Ricardo.

Next day sex was less violent. Just out of the shower, her blond hair fluttered under the hair drier. Ricardo lay supine, silent, head resting on his crossed arms.

Applying the emulsifying cream to her nude body in front of the mirror, she recalled her past.

"My marriage was a big disappointment. He was a musician in a rock band, an unmotivated punk. I was seventeen. Impressionable. What a shitty affair! I left him after a year of a miserable marriage. Luckily, no kids. I vowed to never remarry. I got a sticker for my bumper, Better Dead than Wed."

Mario remained silent enjoying the view.

"I studied nursing. Wrong choice. 'Never gave a shit about the sick and dying, mom. I'm not cut out for that shit,' I told my mother who'd been a nurse once. She cried. I felt sorry later for what I'd said."

"That was strong."

"For lack of anything better and broke, I did nude dancing in San Francisco. At my mother's urge—I hated seeing her shedding tears over me—I went back to college for cooking courses. I worked in kitchens at various levels until I landed a job as a hostess at a famous restaurant in Santa Barbara, California."

"How was it that ya landed in Delsol?" he asked.

"Cause of my husband, Jeremy. He looked very different when he walked into the Maison D'Avignon that evening. Big, tall, tan and bearded under a ten-gallon hat, oozing success down to his alligator leather boots. I opened the door for him and directed him to one of the choice tables. He looked like a good tipper.

"I winked my eye to the waitress as he slid down the booth," she added looking vacantly at the mirror.

"On the way out, he asked for my phone number. He put a one-hundred dollar bill on my hand and said bye."

"So, ya married him for his money."

"Not sure now. Guess I was impressed… Back in Arizona, he kept calling me every day claiming he'd been arrowed by Cupid at first sight. He proposed and I accepted after he'd promised to help me open a restaurant in Delsol."

"That's how ya bought into the Crystal Room."

"Right. But in a few months, there was a turnaround. He morphed into a fat louse. His beer belly exploded. While someone took a gulp, he'd down a 12-pack in a minute."

"And ya hate him now." Ricardo said, lighting up a cigarette.

"Right again. Our sex life went downhill. It sunk to the point all he wanted from me was to rub his humongous gut, or stroke a tiny pecker that I had to find among his belly folds till he went to sleep."

"Ha, ha, ha," he said blowing out a cloud of smoke.

"'That's why I married you,' he'd say with that stinky beer breath before rolling over and going into a thunderous snore."

"I know. Binge drinkers stink."

"Whenever I asked him to take me out to a party with friends or on a nice, romantic dinner, he'd always come up with an excuse: 'Can't miss the ballgame.' Or, 'My friends are coming over.' Or, 'Business meeting with my associates,'" she said, mocking him. "Even, 'The cattle need my attention.' I was always at the bottom of priorities."

Ricardo could not hear her last words. He'd gone to sleep. She approached and yanked the cigarette butt from his fingers and flushed it down the toilet.

On the fourth day of lovemaking, Bonita mentioned her husband's wealth. She had tidied up the room and was dumping the dirty clothing in a hamster.

"I don't want the maids in here. They're nosey and often out-and-out thieves."

"Why don't ya forge his checks? Ya need help? I'm good at that."

"At what?"

"Faking signatures. I've done it before. Best document men couldn't spot the difference. Besides, he wouldn't dare send his own wife to jail."

"No, I got a better idea."

Intrigued, Mario holds his breath.

46

"I know he hasn't written a will. The jerk thinks he's going to live forever."

"What about his relatives?"

"A daughter, Rosemarie. We don't get along."

"That's normal."

"I know he's got a lot of money stashed in banks and bonds. I've gone through his files."

"How much?"

"Lots, lots. Problem's he won't share."

"What's your share?"

"Not much, bastard made me sign a prenuptial agreement."

Next morning, Ricardo surprised Bonita in the kitchen before opening time.

"You look terrible this morning. What's wrong?" she asked.

"My roommate, I almost kicked his ass. Claims I owe him a lot of dough. 'Pay me now or get out of my house!' Guess he expected me paying him back with something."

"A fag?"

"I guess, but he didn't show it before."

After a pause, he continued: "Anyway, came to say goodbye. Going back to Galveston. A trucker's gonna give me a ride." Now he held her by the shoulders. "Kiss me good luck." They kissed.

"You don't need to do that... I mean, leave, Mario," she said cradled in his arms. "You can move into my suite."

"But I'm wiped out. Arabian horses was a lie."

"I knew that. I'm not a country girl."

"You'll get tired of me soon."

"Don't worry about money for now. I've got a way to get rich... together."

That afternoon, Bonita took Ricardo on a ride outside town. She parked half way up a rocky hill with a panoramic view of Delsol below. The fiery sun disk bled the dust clouds crimson before its slide down the horizon. Venomous diamondbacks, rattling, claimed their territory.

The evening smelled of dry desert, succulent cacti, and their blooming flowers.

"I've got a plan. I know how to get at his money—enough to build a brand new diner from the ground up. You could have a piece of it, and realize your dreams."

"What's yer plan, snuff him?"

"I didn't say that. You did."

"Tell me about yer plan, and I'll tell ya if it makes any sense."

"He's finally listened to me. I got him to buy three life insurance policies. Over a million dollars. I'm the sole beneficiary. Nobody's in the know."

"A million," he says, whistling.

"All he needs to do now is kick off."

"Divorce's an option. Have ya thought of it?"

"I have. Divorce would put me on the street. The SOB's got everything on his name—sole and separate. He refuses to buy assets under joint tenancy and he's willing all the assets to Rosemarie 'cause it was his first wife's wish. The only thing we co-own is the car and the plasma TV."

"But, ya've been married to him for years. Ya must still feel something for him."

"Feel? Shoving a giant firecracker up his ass, lighting it and sending him in orbit to outer space, that's how I feel. Can't stand him. Each time he forces himself on me, I wish him dead. Not sure what makes me hate him more, his stinginess or his lovemaking."

"Then, there's no choice?"

"I don't see a way out but bumping the bastard."

They arrived back at the hotel and entered the suite.

"Who's gonna do the number on him?" Ricardo asked.

"We'll both do it. I'll hand him over to you drunk as a skunk. You shoot him dead."

"Hey, w-wait a minute. What's in it for me?"

"You'll get part of the insurance money."

Sitting at the edge of the bed, Ricardo stayed silent for a while. Bonita could not read his thoughts, but suspected greed would triumph.

"Your dreams could become reality. But you have to earn your share," she added.

"I'll tell ya what I want, a condo in Galveston, and some cash to start me out."

"You've got it! Provided after the job, you disappear for good. We can't be seen together. Understand?"

"Business is business. You'll never see me again... unless."

"Pay? Don't worry. As soon as I collect, you'll get your share."

"Better be soon."

"It will. I got a 22 Colt revolver from a reliable friend. Untraceable. I'll show you how to use it. We'll go out to the county for practice. There isn't much to it."

She walked back and forth. Ricardo listened intently.

"It'll be after ten, Texas Eats' closing time. We're the last customers. I make sure he swallows enough beer to doze off a horse. The only thing he notices out of sync's that I'll order more beer for him. He knows I hate the sight and smell of it."

He gives her a vacant look.

"The parking lot'll be deserted. We'll park at the far end, next to your car. You'll wear gloves and dispose of the gun in the trash bin."

"Get rid of him Ricardo, as soon as possible. He's so smashed he won't feel a thing."

"I've never done this... Bump a guy I don't even know."

"Do it!"

"I can't, I can't. My finger's frozen," he whimpered, his hand shaking.

"South of the border... down Mexico way," unsuspecting Jeremy hummed.

"Shoot you son of a bitch or I'll blow your head off and claim you attacked us. That I killed you in self defense!"

She pulled a small Derringer from her purse and pointed it at Ricardo's eyes.

A thud and smoke came out of his gun.

"Do it again. Kill the son of a bitch dead, dead as a doornail... Now run, you idiot. You wanna get caught? Throw the gun in the bin!"

Six months after Jeremy's violent adieu, Bonita finally crowned her ambitions with an eatery that she could proudly call her own child from the ground up. She designed the exterior and interior, the deco, the furniture and the gadgets. She created the menu. She named it the Chez Gourmet and offered to serve, simply, Fine Foods.

Reverent Perry officiated at the grounds' opening and inauguration ceremonies.

She'd gone a long way since her first failed attempt into the food business. She vowed to avoid the mistakes that doomed the Crystal Room a year earlier. She recalled the wise words, "Only fools learn not form past mistakes."

She supervised all aspects of the Chez Gourmet from the time she laid down the first stone. She finally had an establishment commensurate with her dreams, and right from the start, business thrived.

* * *

One year later, a Saturday night, hopping between kitchen and dining room greeting customers and overlooking the operation Bonita looked exhausted, but happy and radiant.

"Ma'am, a Mr Mario Ricardo wants to see you. Says it's urgent."

It was the busiest hour, and when she heard the name from the lips of the hostess, she smirked in displeasure and the sweat pearls on her forehead ran down and stung her eyes.

She removed her apron and came out into the lobby,

"Idiot, I never thought you'd dare coming back," she said, in sotto voce, approaching him.

"Something came up. We need to talk."

"Follow me."

They walked to the back of the restaurant. They entered a workroom with hardly any legroom. A very large old wooden desk occupied almost one half of the office. Two chairs, half-open cabinets cluttered with notebooks, receipts, and files took up the rest of the space.

Wine bottles, ceiling high, were stocked like library tomes against one of the walls. She sat at her work desk. He went around, pulled a chair and sat across her.

"I told you to stay away from here. I kept my part of the bargain."

"And I've kept mine. Haven't been back in over a year, have I?"

"But now you're fucking with me. What is it? Spit it out."

"Things have turned to shit. I love gambling. Lost the condo in a bad binge at the cards. Lisa and kids have gone to her mother's. I've got no place to stay," he said, swinging his head like a weathercock.

"Nothing to do with me."

"Don't get me wrong," he said, with a smirk.

"Thought of everything, but running out of choices I decided to rekindle an old friendship."

"What the fuck do you want?"

"What do I want?" he said, looking down her neckline.

"Don't even dream of it! That's history. Buried. Period."

"I need some dough to keep me goin'."

"More? We had a contract."

"Contract? Don't remember any contract. Besides, new contingencies've come up." And entertained by the stack of wine bottles, he added, "I've got a nose for fine wine… and money."

"Okay, okay, I got you, but on one condition—your ass disappears from my life for good."

"That's perfectly okay with me."

"You'll get five grand. That's it."

She pulled the checkbook out of the drawer and wrote down a check. "I think you've been overpaid. You were a louse in bed and a big fuck-up that night."

She tore it off from the book angrily and tossed it his way. He tore it to pieces and tossed it sideways.

"Shit, that's peanuts!"

"W-what?"

"Look lady, I've learned a lot since then. I'm not stupid. I know what I'm worth. Five grand's nothing. I want ya to buy me another house, then, I'll get Lisa back."

"A house! Ha, ha, ha. You're crazy. That costs a bundle. Property's gone up lately."

"But ya can afford it," he said opening his arms to demonstrate her wealth… Anyway, the alternative's unthinkable, ain'it? Ya, spending a lifetime in jail? Can't even imagine it," he added with a twisted smirk.

"You mean you'd go to the cops? You'd hang yourself, you idiot."

"I don't care. Rather die in prison than live in poverty and without Lisa and the kids."

"That's crap! When did you give a fuck about your wife and kids?"

"Believe it or not I've got a heart," he said patting his chest, "And it can be touched by love and tenderness… "

"Don't bullshit me," she said.

Menacing, leaning across the table, he continued, "Look lady, I want ya to come over to my town and search for property. I'm not gonna wait long, I warn ya. Here's my particulars. Ya can find me at this motel." Getting up, he tossed her a sticky note.

51

Bonita showed Ricardo the way out through the service door.

A few minutes later, the receptionist forwarded a phone call to Bonita. She was still in her office, stunned by the recent visit. She picked up the receiver.

"Darius from The Vermin Hitmen."

"Darius? I don't need your services yet. You did a good job last time. The place's clean," she said.

"That's not exactly why I called," he said. After a pause, he continued:

"Have you followed the news on your husband's shooting?"

"No, have they found a suspect?"

"Not exactly, but the police revealed the murder weapon—a 22 Colt revolver. It was in the news this morning."

There was another pause punctuated by Bonita's laborious breathing.

"Same kind of gun I got you few days before the shooting," he continued.

A tension-packed pause followed.

"Look, we've gotta talk. How about lunch at twelve tomorrow?" she asked.

Darius kept the appointment. Bonita welcomed him into a private corner booth away from view and noise in the busy dining room. Fine food was part of her strategy. She sat in front of him and ordered lunch for two. He picked Rack of Lamb at her suggestion. He opened the conversation.

"The news sent chills up my spine. There's an ugly shooting and it turns out the gun's the same type I've got for you. Too much of a coincidence. Tell me I'm wrong."

"And you want to sell me your silence?"

"I wouldn't put it that crudely. But I'm taking a great risk."

"I'm ready to offer you a deal. Fifty grand will settle it, but you must do a job for me."

"What kind of job?"

"Look, you're a good vermin exterminator. There's vermin I need to take care of."

The waiter approached, took the wine order and left.

"Let's toast, then we'll talk," she said.

After the appetizer, there came the buttered fresh-baked bread, the sliced, marinated beef tongue, the bowl of Caesar salad.

Then came the main entre, the house specialty. Darius ate the whole thing and then licked the rib bones and his fingers. Bonita ordered more lamb. Over a glass of cognac, Bonita handed him a fat envelope.

"Glad to do business with you," she said, lifting her glass. She pulled an old driver license Ricardo had left behind and the sticky note he had given her the previous day and handed them over to Darius.

"Here's what you get now, the other half, later," she said.

He peeked into the envelope and read the note, and his eyes widening, he whistled letting a smile creep up his face.

Darius had considered several of his friends and acquaintances for the job. He eliminated most prospects. He couldn't bet that they wouldn't run to the cops and squeal about the plan to eliminate Ricardo.

Navarro was different. The explosives expert at the old copper mine—now closed—where they both once worked, often played cover for him when he cheated on his wife. He could count on his confidentiality. Navarro had lost his job. Ten grand came like manna from heaven. Bumping off somebody 1000 miles away was safe and seemingly a slam-dunk.

He had no problem finding Mario Ricardo in Galveston.

He stalked him for two days and studied his movements and daily routine. Before sunrise of the third day, he hid a powerful pipe bomb under the car's chassis, and set it to explode at the turn of the ignition switch.

He observed, unseen, from a safe distance as Ricardo walked out of his motel room accompanied by a woman.

She's not part of the bargain. Sorry for her, but little can be done now, Navarro mumbled.

He saw the couple approaching the car and Ricardo pointing an ignition remote at the front door. The tremendous explosion shook Navarro to the bones and left him numb and deaf. He decided to put as much distance between him and the site as possible. He landed on the driver's seat and sped back to the highway, westbound.

He knew the effects of dynamite on the human anatomy, but decided not to think about the mangled flesh he'd left behind.

Ricardo and his wife spent a day in the ER of the hospital and were discharged with a lot of scratches but no serious injuries.

Looking out the window of the taxi stopped for a red light, Ricardo happened to read the headlines on the local paper displayed at an intersection's booth.

"Local couple miraculously survive tremendous car bombing," he read.

"That was Bonita's job. I told ya to be careful with that bitch while ya were fuckin' her," Lisa Ricardo said.

"She'll pay for this. I swear."

"What're ya gonna do?"

"I'll think of something."

"I ain't waiting no more. Not gonna have the kids hurt. I'll ask for police protection."

"Hush woman, yer crazy. Ya go to the cops, I'll kill ya," he said into her ear.

Empty words in her opinion. If I must choose between kids and husband, choice couldn't be clearer to me.

She did go to the cops and they arrested Ricardo.

She knew all the details of Burn's sacrifice as Ricardo had taken her into his confidence. She stayed behind with the kids and started divorce proceedings.

* * *

Bonita, Darius, and his wife were having Rack of Lamb in a corner of the restaurant. They were laughing and tipsy after the champagne and wine. At the end of the last toast, he handed him a fat envelope. He smiled and put it in his pocket.

Det Maravilla, accompanied by two blues, interrupted the celebration. He recited the Miranda rights at the head of the table.

"Mrs Burns, Mario Ricardo's waved extradition from Galveston and is now detained in Delsol County Jail. He's given us a detailed account of the conspiracy to kill your husband. You're under arrest for capital murder."

"That's impossible. He's, he's d—"

"Mr Darius, you're in for conspiracy and attempted murder."

"You idiot, give me back my money!" she said, snatching the envelope from Darius' hand.

"That's ours. Evidence," Maravilla said, jerking the envelope from her.

The officers yanked them from their booth seats and cuffed them. Mrs Darius started to cry.

Mr Darius went away subdued and willingly, but Bonita was carried away kicking and screaming.

Ricardo got death. Darius pled guilty and got ten years in lockup. Navarro got twenty for attempted murder. Bonita hired a competent and expensive defense team that, in the end, could not bend the jury in her favor. The verdict was guilty and she received a life sentence without the possibility of parole. Unable to come to terms with her loss of freedom, she committed suicide one year later swallowing rat bait smuggled into the prison by Rosemarie.

4. DEBITS AND OBITS

My name's Joe Maravilla of the Delsol Police Department-Homicide. Memorial Day, year 20xx, I received a call on my cruiser from the dispatcher about a missing high school girl. Most personnel were on leave and I was the only lawman available.

"Last time we saw her? Last Friday night. She stood by that door and said, 'I'm going to a slumber party.'"

"What time Friday?" I asked pulling out my notebook.

"Must've been around eight…" she said clearing her throat.

"Go on Mrs Sword," I said, sitting across her and Mr Sword, parents of the disappeared, in the living room of a modest but well-decorated house in a working class district of Delsol, Arizona.

Visibly distraught, she continued: "I asked my daughter, 'What time will you be back?' 'Don't wait for me mom. Melissa'll drop me back in the morning,' she answered."

I wrote down the name. First lead.

"Who's Melissa?" I asked.

"A classmate. The one hosting the slumber party."

It took her a few seconds to regain her composure.

"I didn't want her to leave. I told her I had a bad premonition. She laughed it off, 'All my school friends'll be there,' she said.

" 'Call Melissa's mom if you don't believe me,' she added and gave me Melissa's phone number. 'I'll be okay,' were her last words with one foot out the door."

She started sobbing.

I decided to wait a couple minutes, then, I continued the questioning after I took down Melissa's phone number.

"What happened then?"

"Melissa's car had just pulled up with a bunch of boys and girls. Natasha'd seen it through the living room drapes.

"She hurried out and jumped in the back seat. I couldn't see their faces."

"Can you give me names of people your daughter associates with?"

Mrs Sword blew her nose with the Kleenex and came up with two more female names, then she said, "We called Melissa and her mother and they told us they hadn't seen our daughter since the party."

"Your daughter. What does she look like?" I asked.

Mrs Sword crossed the carpeted room to a side table and grabbed a picture frame. She put it in my hands.

"She's freckled, fair skinned, auburn hair, brown eyes, average size, straight-A student... till recently."

"She's a great kid. The life of varsity volleyball. Most Valuable Player last year," added Mr Sword, a retired machinist.

"We were so proud of her," continued Mrs Sword.

"Why did you say 'Till recently'?" I asked.

"A few months ago, after she turned eighteen, we noticed a change."

"About the time those punks came into her life," said Mr Sword, gravely.

"Can you come up with some names?" I asked.

"Ricky Snapps and the other one, B—Bu," stuttered Mrs Sword.

"Butch Snyper. In my days we'd take them scumbags and sink their heads in the toilet. I warned those SOBs to stay away from my daughter..."

"Please John, upset's bad for your heart. Besides, we don't know anything yet," pled the lady.

I saw why Mr Sword was unhealthy. He was not the type to take things lightly. I put down the names on paper.

"She loved volleyball," he said.

"When the coach removed her from the team, she was devastated," added Mrs Sword.

"We noticed a change. Missed classes, bad grades, school notices. There were other warning signs," added Mr Sword.

"She started spending full nights out, weekends first, then weekdays too. We tried to talk to her, but she was evasive.

"We even grounded her a few times but she'd slip out at midnight through a bedroom window."

"I warned Butch to stay away from her and our house," snapped the gentleman. "We haven't seen that punk for weeks. I think he knows her whereabouts," he added, breathing heavily.

I sympathized with them and tried to comfort them, "A missing child's a terrible thing to go through. When young people disappear, they're usually hiding with friends. We'll check 'em all out," I said replacing my notebook in my pocket.

There was no more I could do at that time.

"Let me know the minute you hear some news or she turns up, will you?" I said handing them my card and crossing to the door.

As I mounted my car, I reached for my cellular and started making calls. This case took several turns. Subsequent investigations and accounts from witnesses revealed the following scenario. I took the liberty of filling up the gaps to make some sense out of a senseless chain of events.

Ricky Snapps, a handsome senior with Hollywood looks, met Butch Snyper a few weeks before Natasha's disappearance on the campus of Van Horne High School. Two punk girls flanked Butch. One, tall, strong, brunette wore extreme black make-up and a black halter and jeans. With lipstick the color of dry blood, Ricky imagined her a disciple of Dracula. Her companion, a petite blond, looked gaunt and ashen and wore cheap diamonds on her belly button. She had the looks of a starved and sleep-deprived POW and seemed to relish on the image. Both of them, scantily dressed, had tattoos over their breasts.

"Whatcha lookin' at," Butch asked, annoyed. "Ya wanna have our portraits?"

"Just wandering if I'd met you before… someplace," Ricky said grinning with the tameness of a pack dog running into the alpha dog.

"Maybe we have. He looks familiar," said POW.

"And he's cute too," added the black-clad girl.

After a tense pause everybody relaxed.

"Whatcha dig, coffee or tea?" Butch asked in a happier tone. Ricky stood speechless and ashamed of being so naive and inexperienced.

"Ha, ha, ha, he's afraid. Why don't we leave him alone?" said Black.

"Yeah, let him have his milk," said POW, as if part of a chorus.

"Cluck, cluck, cluck," went Black, doing the chicken impersonation. Butch and his escorts had a laugh, turned and walked away.

"Hey, w-wait, here's some money. Give me coffee and milk and whatever you've got," said Ricky, pulling out his wallet. This was the beginning of a fateful friendship.

The group made a strong impression on Ricky and he vowed to meet them again and try to buy his membership into their club. He was rewarded some days later when he was accepted into their circle.

Ricky and Butch couldn't be more diverse but they came to need each other.

With Ricky, money was no factor. He provided the gadgets, the red Corvette, the expensive booze, the catering and the sound for the parties.

Butch knew where the wrong girls were and provided the drugs, which was great as far as Ricky was concerned. Butch's girls fascinated him. His mother-approved ones bored him to death.

Butch Snyper was the poster image of the school pusher. Drooping shouldered, acne-scarred, jaundiced, his hair crew-cut like a mule's mane, he liked to brag about his exploits:

"Paint sniffer at eight, pothead at ten, acidhead at 12, tweeker at 14, pusher at 17. My pa, a truck driver, stays away. Each time he comes home, he looks more like a stranger. My ma does stay back, but she's seldom home."

He claimed student status but nobody had seen him sitting in classrooms; yet, his presence was a normal sight on campus. He materialized wherever, whenever anybody needed a fix. He set up business at the school cafeteria. A major dealer drafted him. Being a minor of student age, he was a good front for the ring's activities. Through Butch, they peddled drugs among the students, on and off the school.

Ricky met Reba Snyper soon after his first encounter with her son, Butch. He dropped at her home unannounced. Reba answered the door.

"He's not home, who are you?"

"I'm Ricky, friend from school, and you?"

"Reba, Butch's mother."

Wow, mother? I expected a plump fifty-something, gray hair rolled up in a bun. I find a foxy chick with a head full of red blown hair and sex oozing out of her pores! he thought.

"Come on in hon," she said, beckoning him into the waiting room, "He'll be back soon."

"Thanks… be back later… after all, didn't call first," he said, embarrassed and eager to run away like a child urged to pee.

"Okay hon. I'll tell him you dropped by."

The next day, I called Mrs Sword. "Ma'am, I've checked all of your daughter's friends. No signs of her yet. Nobody knows her whereabouts. We're upgrading this to a missing person case and widening the search."

Two more days passed and nobody had heard from Natasha. Rumors traveled fast. The Delsol Herald broke up the news in large black letters, front page: MYSTERIOUS DISAPPEARANCE OF LOCAL TEEN.

Dozens of lawmen and volunteers canvassed the town, the hang outs where Natasha might have been, the school grounds, vacant lots, even the city dump. Nothing.

I summoned Ricky Snapps to the prescient again.

After two hours of questioning he didn't change his story:

"I don't have an idea where she might be. I spent day and night at my friend Butch Snyper's house listening to music and playing computer games," he said.

Butch was next. He came accompanied by his mother, Reba Snyper. His story and Ricky's matched up. Mrs Snyper corroborated their alibis.

"I'm sure these kids'd nothing to do with that girl's disappearance. That Friday, they were at my home all day and night," Reba declared.

Without any evidence to the contrary, I had to let the youths go.

"But you mustn't leave town. I might be calling back if Miss Sword doesn't turn up," I added out the door.

Mr Snyper's trade kept him away weeks at a time. Yet, glands didn't take long vacations. So Reba Snyper couldn't help feeling excited each time Ricky dropped by to pay a visit to her son Butch.

Reba looked through a peephole bored by Butch through the bathroom wall to ogle his sister's unaware girlfriends.

She eyeballed chisel-bodied Ricky taking showers.

"I've gotta have that," she said once so loudly that Ricky could hear her over the cascading water.

One day Ricky showed up unannounced. This time he knew Butch wasn't home.

Reba welcomed him naked under a bath towel wrapped tight around hips and breasts. Fire sparkled back and forth. She insisted that he came in and waited for Butch. He cheerfully accepted. He sat on the couch.

"Make yourself comfortable. Going for a shower. Mind if I leave you alone?"

He said he wouldn't and sunk into the sofa. She smiled coquettishly and left the room. He examined the posters on the walls. *Paintings of nude men and women like those found in bordellos,* he thought. She reappeared minutes later soaked wet and sans the towel.

She approached Ricky and grabbed him by the hand. The king-sized bed fitted in Reba's alcove with room to spare. The carpet was passion red, her walk-in closet, wall-stacked with fashions and shoes. Negligees of different colors lay around chairs like sitting guests. A full-size ceiling mirror over the bed. A large poster with a legend pasted to the wall.

She led him to the round bed in the center of the alcove and wrestled his clothes off. He felt like a train had passed over him. As she slithered to the bathroom, he pinned his eyes on the wall poster:

KINGSIZE BED
Avid mouths screaming out
Reptile brain's moaning sounds.
Linen sheets tossed around,
Naked bodies amok,
Like fast hands of a clock
Turning on the kingsize bed.
Fingers pulling at the sheets
And teeth sinking into flesh.
Fingers tearing at the flesh.
Stained covers, wrinkled spreads,
Underpants torn to shreds
Soiling the kingsize bed.
Brain-crippling catatonic flashes

And lust and adrenaline rushes
Banging on the kingsize bed.
Rock-boat of pleasure and pain.
Too much for the human brain,
Too much for the kingsize bed.

He came up with another erection. Reba returned from the bathroom and found him standing up, like a one-arm saguaro tree.

"You like it? I wrote it and had a poster made," she said. They jumped back in bed.

A few days later Ricky and Reba were balling in bed while her husband was away driving the truck.

"He doesn't mind. We have an understanding," she said, addressing his concerns about Mr Snyper's reactions to their affair.

Naked and spread-eagled in bed, they ogled each other in the ceiling mirror. Like a snake by the head, she stroke and shook his rod, hardly listening to him, but rather concentrating on her own agenda. That particular day he hadn't enjoyed the up and down.

He was uneasy, consumed by anxiety.

For months Ricky had kept a secret locked up in his mind, but the pangs of remorse were becoming intolerable.

That day he decided to unload his conscience on Reba, now his lover and confidant, but he found it hard to get the words out.

"I was ten but I remember it like yesterday. That Christmas, father took us to visit Grandpa."

"Christmas? Ho, ho, ho," she went, like Santa.

"We drove all the way to his ranch house in New Mexico. Surrounded by sheets of white snow, like a plantation mansion, it had three stories and dozens of windows. The brick chimney spitted gray smoke when we arrived.

"Felt cool coming back to this grandiose house after some years. I'd seen nothing but snow for miles and felt thrills at the front door. My aunts—pair of fatsos—welcomed us inside. They grabbed my mother by the shoulders and kissed, kissed, kissed. They turned their attentions to me."

Wiping his mouth in disgust, he continued: "I hated it. They called me little baby and smooched me with their fat, wet mouths. I wiped my cheeks and cursed them."

"I'll smooch you to death," Reba said, kissing him on the chest.

"After the initial joy and all the long-time-no-see's, they led us to a screened patio back of the house. Grandpa sat there accompanied by one of his farmhands. Big happy Brenda lay next to him licking his boots with an attitude like, 'I wanna participate and be helpful, oink, oink.'"

"Who's Brenda?"

"A real big pig grandpa'd raised since birth. Everybody treated her like family. Free to come in and out and roam inside at will. She'd jump on the sofa and watch TV with the kids. The happiest pig I'd ever seen!"

"Oink, oink."

"With all the excellent food and preferential treatment, she could be considered in the best of physical shape and spirits. She felt like part of the family," he continued, his blink-less eyes pinned to the ceiling mirror.

"Grandpa was in his 90's but much younger looking—an old lecher still craving for young flesh. Ma and Pa used to make fun of him. 'Never mind my age, I don't plan to kick off any time soon,' he bragged."

"I'd like to meet him," Reba said.

"Everything he put into his mouth, meat or vegetable, he raised himself in his ranch. He was a freak for organic crap."

"Hey, don't make fun. I like organic bananas."

Refusing to get out of his reverie, he continued:

"'We're gonna have roast for dinner,' Grandpa announced that day."

Ricky didn't mind talking into dead ears. He kept yapping while Reba slithered down the bed and grabbed Ricky's tool and applied to it her avid lips. Patiently, Reba tried again and again ignoring Ricky's words. Failing to revive Ricky's limp tool, she lay again by his side.

"What happened next kind of shocked me, maybe 'cuz I'm no country boy. Grandpa fastened the end of a rope around the pig's leg and the other end to a nearby tree while the farmhand held a second rope around her neck and pulled at it.

"First, the pig radiated happiness. She went along with it. Guess she thought they were playing a tease game. Except the game was getting rough and rougher. Next, Grandpa took a long butcher's knife from a nearby table and cut the pig's jugular.

"When she refused to die he stabbed her in the heart. It took long for Brenda to die, or so I thought. The pig's howling and all the blood gushing out stunned me. It splattered grandpa's arms and overalls and stained everything crimson red.

"Her howls were deafening. More than feeling pain the desperate pig seemed to ask: 'Why're you doing this to me? Aren't you friends, family?'

"I felt nauseated and left the scene. I went back into the house and tried to block it out of my mind."

"Oink, oink," said Reba in Ricky' ear. He recoiled.

"Reba, it's no laughing matter."

"Oink, oink."

"That night, at dinnertime, lots of friends and relatives sat around the gigantic oak dinner table. Others drank and toasted all over the house while I sat by the family room's fireplace."

Ricky sweated profusely, as if sitting by a bonfire in summertime.

"Dinner's served!" one of my aunts yelled. Everybody ate from Brenda's carcass that lay in the middle of the table on a large silver tray. 'Browned with my secret BBQ sauce and roasted slowly over an ironwood fire. Happy pigs are best-tasting pigs,' Grandpa mouthed off.

"'Why did you kill your pet, grandpa?' I asked. 'Wasn't my pet, son. I raised it for food. Fed her the best stuff so she'd taste good,' that's how he shrugged it off. I refused to eat that night. My mother asked if I felt sick. I said I wasn't hungry."

Reba didn't listen. There were more important things to think about that night. She continued stroking his rod, like she did between sex bouts. Still no erection.

Impatient, she lay back along Ricky. Irritated, she waggled his rod like a gearlever. He shrank back in pain and tossed her hand away.

"Ouch! Take it easy. It hurts."

"What's wrong with you? Don't you like me any more?"

"You know that's not it."

"I bet you've just been with someone. Who's she? One of those little whores at Horny Hi?"

"Van Horne Hi, and stop the shit. Shut up and listen. Got something to tell you."

They sat up face-to-face in the manner of couples trying to redefine their relationship after a lovers' spat.

Later, they lay back down side-to-side, eyes nailed to the ceiling mirror.

"The end of last May, school was over. We'd finished finals and partying and orgying was on everybody's mind. The demand for smokeshit reached its peak. Even those who pretended not to dig it thought it was cool for the occasion. Butch could hardly meet the demand. He arrived on campus to make deliveries and we met.

"He asked if I had seen Natasha that day. I said I did and knew where to find her—at Melissa's slumber party. He said he wanted to talk to her, that she owed him a lot of dough, 'She likes the best and purest stuff, you know, and collection time's overdue. Suppliers are getting nervous and over demanding. I must have a rattle with her, in private.'

I offered my home since Old Fart and Ma had headed for California to visit Sis. I called Natasha on her cell phone and asked her to wait outside for us. She agreed."

Reba's joy started to turn to annoyance.

"We told her I was throwing a party at my home and that a lot of our mutual friends'd be there. 'Awesome!' she said and came along. The three of us got on Butch's Mustang. He parked in the garage and we entered. Nobody saw us. My house is on a big lot secluded from neighbors by big shade trees.

"She noticed the lack of guests. We explained they'd crash in later. She smiled, sat down, and asked for some booze. I fixed a banger and poured extra stuff in it. She liked it and drank it up like soda pop. I fixed us another and another and after a while we were all shitfaced."

"Who's that Natasha?" asked Reba.

"That girl Sword who disappeared last summer."

"But Butch told me you both spent the night driving around, chatting, listening to music."

"By the way, we can't thank you enough for covering up for us."

Reba drew back and hugged herself as if in a sudden chill.

"Tell me all about it. Then, what happened?" she asked.

"Butch demanded payment for the dope he'd given her, 'I know you're sharing it with boyfriends, you pig,' he accused her…

"'Payback time's now.'

"'You said it was a gift. I don't owe you a penny.' She said.

"'Never said that, you lying bitch.'

"Butch was pissed at Natasha taking too many free samples. He had his obligations. She'd become a heavy user of quality stuff. She owed. He often suggested she borrow or steal from relatives and friends or even rob a store to pay her debt, but she shrugged it all off and never paid a cent. That night, she offered to pay with sex."

Reba, curled up in a fetal position, remained silent.

"The party went on. We sniffed the melting stuff from a metal spoon over a flame. She enjoyed that. Next, we took off our clothes. Me first, then Butch. First, she dug it and I could see her enjoying it, or at least didn't voice any complaint.

"I thought that was the highlight of the night. Screwing a good-looking little bitch, getting a couple of blowjobs, laughing it all away, and taking her back home.

"But Butch wanted to go anal. He grabbed her from behind. She objected, 'You're hurting me!' she screamed. We laughed it off. I grabbed her by the arms while Butch performed the penetration. She screamed. We took turns with the sodomizing. She begged for mercy but we didn't have no pity. Then she broke loose and fought back. He slapped and overpowered her.

"'Get me some twine,' he said, and I got him some hemp rope from the garage. He fastened her arms to the heavy metal bed."

"You're making all this up. My Butch wouldn't…"

"It's the truth, I swear. And like Judas, I handed her over to him," he said.

"It's not true!" she said.

"Butch's a sadist. He loves to inflict pain. As young as eleven he liked to catch squirrels, 'Douse them with kerosene and light 'em up,' he told me once, 'I got kicks out of their desperate squeals.'"

"Watch what you're saying."

He went on oblivious to her protests.

"Butch tied a noose around her neck and started pulling with all his strength. She griped loudly during the process but the chocking drowned down her screams. She was strong. She wouldn't pass out easily."

"Not true…" Reba sobbed.

"Then, in spite of my stupor, I realized we were going too far…

"I retired to the far end of the room and told Butch to take it easy. He would not listen but laughed it off. She was bleeding and screaming. He stopped the sexual attack and went to serious business."

"Stop that."

"She begged for her life 'Please stop. Please stop. It hurts too much!'

"'Payback time!' he said."

"Impossible. Butch isn't capable of hurting a fly. I know my son," Reba said, uncurling, mother hen instinct in full swing.

"Mothers are the last to know their real sons. I was dumbstruck. Saw him kill a cat, hang it with piano wire, but murder? Never entered my mind!"

"Don't believe you. My Butch ain't capable of murder," Reba said, contentiously.

Ricky went on, under the spell of his recollections.

"I was stunned. Couldn't comprehend what Butch had done. It wasn't in my plans to kill anybody. It happened so suddenly. He'd planned it for weeks. I remembered his words: 'I dreamed I choked a girl to death and it felt so good.'

"Why didn't you stop him?" she said, wiping tears.

"I couldn't stand it, ran to the bathroom and puked. When I got back he was feeling her neck veins and breath. She was dead. We smoked the meth pipe. I just wanted to get rid of her. Was afraid for my parents, friends, the scandal. What happened next is kind of blurry, like a pipe dream."

Reba keeps whimpering.

"I helped him wrap her in blankets and carry her out. The kitchen opened directly into the garage. We locked her in the trunk of his Mustang and drove southwards towards Horny Goat Pass. In the black and misty night Butch found a hidden ravine beyond the liquor bottles and beer cans of the night before's partying. We unloaded her and placed her on the ground."

She continues sobbing.

"He pulled a can from the trunk and poured gas on her and lit her up. He watched the pyre from a distance. 'Ha, ha, ha, you bitch. You won't steal from me no more,' he snickered.

"But incredibly, the corpse recoiled and sat up. 'Aaaah!' she screamed…

"He burnt her alive! He picked up a branch of ironwood and banged her on the head while the flames hissed and popped. The bonfire lit the night. I feared the flames would attract someone. Then the fire consumed itself down to a dark mound and bright ambers. 'She's changed, beautiful no more, just charcoal,' he said, with a diabolical grin.

"With the flames self-extinguishing, he pulled a shovel from the car, dug a shallow hole in the ground and rolled her in. He covered it with dirt and dead branches. Sweat soaked and dusty but satisfied, he returned to the car."

Reba hides her head in her arms.

"I'm scared, I said. What will my parents say? I couldn't stand the shame of confronting 'em. And her parents? That'll be even worse.

'Nobody'll ever know,' he said, 'and we'll go on with our lives.' He's been back to the grave several times claiming he loved her. He placed flowers on her grave last week.

"Since that day, I cannot live with myself. I have nightmares. A pig with Natasha's face snarls and chases me and I wake up sweaty and breathless," Ricky finished, rolling into a fetal position.

"Butch ain't capable of something like that. You're trying to put the blame on him to save your own hide, you son of a bitch." she explodes, pouncing on him.

"Ouch! You've cut me, you hysterical bitch!" he cries, in tears. He wipes the red oozing out of three slashes running down his right cheek. Blood keeps sipping out of the cuts.

"Get out of my house before I yell rape!"
Bouncing out of bed, he slips his jeans on and double-times out. "Fuck you!" he screams, disappearing out the front door.

Reba recovered. Her brain went on overdrive. She would place all the blame on Ricky. After all, he was 19 and her son only 17, an innocent minor in her eyes and the eyes of the law. She hurried to the police department and asked for the homicide detective in charge of the Natasha case. I directed her to my office.

She swore that Ricky had confessed to the murder of Natasha adding garnishings of her own, but with a twist; that her son had been coerced by Ricky to go along with him and help dispose of the body.

"Ricky Snnaps has confessed to the murder of Natasha Sword...

"I've just heard the whole story from his own mouth. My son was there, but had nothing to do with it. Butch's a minor, only 16 when this happened. He was coerced by Ricky to go along with him and help dispose of the body. Ricky has revealed the grave's location. Horny Goat Pass, where it meets the creek."

I typed her declaration and had her sign it; then, I sprang up from my chair.

"Mrs Snyper, I'm going to ask you to accompany me to the site, and please, keep what we've discussed here confidential, will you?"

I gathered the homicide and forensic teams and rocketed to Horny Goat Pass and quickly found the grave. Rocks piled up in the form of a body. Fresh flowers over the dirt mound.

The prosecution opened with the medical examiner's report: Blunt force trauma to head and shoulders, broken neck, smoke in lungs. Still alive when set on fire.

Natasha's relatives occupied the first row at the trial. They wept and Mrs Sword, with feeble legs, helped out by his son Billy, had to leave the courtroom at the end of the autopsy report.

Melissa declared before the court television cameras that she had seen Natasha leave that night with an older guy that she could not identify as it was too dark outside.

The counsel resorted to the blame-the-drugs-for-behavior defense. The guilty verdict came quickly. The sentences were lenient due to Ricky's top-notch and expensive attorneys and Butch's age, coupled with the latter one's alleged secondary role in the crime. The jury agreed on one point, Ricky had been the perpetrator and Butch, the catalyst.

They met a sympathetic judge. Second-degree murder. He sentenced Ricky to ten years in state prison, and Butch, to Juvenile till his 21st birthday. The faces of the accused and defense counsels lit up in joy and disbelief. Relatives of the accused left the courtroom relieved and contented and kissing each other, but a second family, the Swords, left in tears of disappointment.

Natasha's family protested the light sentences for such a heinous crime, but their pleas were ignored. Rumors ran that the judge and the jury foreman's hands had been handsomely buttered.

Natasha's brother, Billy Sword, vowed to take revenge and developed a plan—spurred by his father—to stalk Ricky in the cellblocks.

St Angel State Prison Warden's hands were also friendly to butter. Billy was hired as a guard in Ricky's cellblock.

The guards didn't have a high opinion of their work place. Prison personnel had a high turnover rate. The Civil Liberties Union lambasted St Angel State Prison due to "The high number of casualties among the inmates. And a climate of fear that amounts to cruel and unusual punishment," it said, through its spokesman.

The warden, taking issue with the statements from the CLU, retorted, "The fact-finding report of the Bureau of Prisons declared St Angel State Prison the most problematic of detention facilities with the greatest population of dangerous felons in the national detention system.

"Death-row-ites and lifers are always on the prowl for targets of opportunity to quench an insatiable thirst for blood. Inmates slash each other with shanks over the theft of a toothbrush. Despite our best efforts to prevent it, bloodletting is the aftermath of escapes from Maximum Security into the general population. The solution is more money and more personnel, not untrained criticism from the outside."

Ricky Snapps didn't have to share his tiny but comfortable cage at St. Angel State Prison. They kept him always at a safe distance from the general population. Even while showering, guards closely watched him and escorted him back to his cell. They left him alone only after locked up securely and the keys stashed in a safe place in the guardhouse.

He had to thank his parents as well as the rest of his blood-relatives and influential friends for this privilege. His kin had owned, for generations, thousands of acres of pastureland and heads of cattle numbering in the six figures.

Ricky cried almost every day since the first day of his incarceration, "Why am I caged in a place like this? The lawyers, the DA, even the governor had promised me help."

He exasperated inmates in the cellblock with his whining, often lasting through the night. He'd spend hours terrified and curled up in a fetal position in a corner of his cell. For someone who'd been advantaged and pampered all his life, there was no way he could come to terms with his internment in a facility holding a hardcore criminal element.

"The dregs of society," newspapers cackled…

"Impervious to any concept of humanity or rehabilitation."

His over-paid lawyers were speeding an appeal, and lobbying everybody from the presiding judge to the prison's warden, the state's attorney general, and even the state governor for privileges and protection for the rich young scion.

* * *

Three am, Christmas morning, two guards materialized out of the tarmac in front of Ricky's cell. The date, the time, and the ominous rumors that wafted in the prison like a foul odor presaged evil. He was petrified.

The tall one, six-six, lanky, stooped, was never known to smile. He unlocked the metal door and entered while his companion stood outside as a lookout. Ricky recognized him in the penumbra of the cell. He was unforgettable—tall, freckled, pink skinned, child-faced.

"Billy Sword! What're you doing here?" Ricky exclaimed, surprised.

"Move. We're taking you for a ride," Billy said, economical with words. Billy pulled out flex cuffs, tied Ricky's hands and sealed his mouth with duct tape. So restrained, the guards lifted him from the floor where he had buckled down in a fruitless attempt to resist.

They took him across the halls past several cellblocks. They unlocked and locked back barred gates till they reached a dark and deserted laundry warehouse that smelled strongly of bleach. The washers and driers remained silent, subdued and resting from the daily punishment of the dirty laundry.

They dropped him in the middle of the warehouse like a mail parcel bag.

The guards walked away and stood inconspicuously against the room wall leaving a panicked Ricky wriggling and struggling to get up from his untenable position.

Seconds later, a side door opened with a cringing sound of rusted hinges. Known in prison as the Sex Wackos, six convicts in the height of prison fashion careened into the room and went to it efficiently, mechanically, as if working from a script.

The governor's investigation was nasty. The warden and several guards gave their version of the events in interrogation rooms in front of police and federal agents. Inmates were lured with deals, others threatened with the heavy arm of the law in exchange for the truth.

The silent ones were secretly waterboarded to turn them more conversational. All members of the murdering gang were identified and submitted to grueling hours of segregation and interrogation. With the information obtained, the authorities built up a virtual reality scenario. The self-appointed leader of the Sex Wackos sang like a diva:

"First, we made some bows and curtsies in the direction of our audience, the guards, in the manner of ballerinas from the Nutcracker. Then we surrounded the hog-tied man, removed his clothes and turned him into the star of the lowest, dirtiest porno show.

"All of us took turns sodomizing him until blood gushed out of his orifices. Then, we held him and made him give us flute jobs. Next we made him punk on his knees. Each time a sound came out of his mouth, we kicked him about the torso till his ribs cracked. After about an hour of this medication, we let him rest on the floor where he'd collapsed. Then, Big Bill, the guard who orchestrated the show said, 'He's had enough. Go to plan B.'

"We lifted the guy up, tied a noose made out of bed sheets around his neck, pulled him up, and hanged him from a ceiling beam until he did the ballet-kick finale. We were baffled that he'd died smiling as if death had been a blessing.

"Both of them guards watched the number. Big Bill, leaning against the wall, stood immobile and poker-faced. Shorty, the small, dark guard, on the contrary, wriggled and giggled. 'He, he, he. He, he, he,' he snickered all the time. I faced the guards and said, 'Thanks for the treat,' while my buddies grinned through their windowed dentures. We gathered ourselves and went quietly away.

"Next morning, the laundry open for business, the sight of Billy's body swinging from the ceiling—a blood-soaked human candelabrum—touched a chord in the hardest-hearted inmates.

"We heard the body was put inside a bag, on top of a gurney, and carried away. They laid it on the platform in the autopsy room and sliced it from top to bottom. The jail doctor wrote down the cause of death. He was placed on ice and readied for pick up by relatives. The usual shit, I heard.

"We followed the news. The guy's parents picked him up and insisted on accompanying the body aboard the funerary limousine. Unfortunately, they were t-boned by a drunk driver in a pickup...

"The mother died of an exploded spleen on her way to the hospital and the father was paralyzed from the waist down. There was a double funeral. Sad, sad, sad."

Further interrogations, like pieces of a puzzle, exposed the scenario that culminated in Ricky's final adieu. The culprits were given what they deserved. The warden was demoted to Guard Class-One.

Billy Sword, alias Big Bill, and Shorty were arrested and charged with first-degree murder. All of the Sex Wackos were placed at the disposal of the merciless courts.

5. I'M A DOCTOR

At Roma Bella, a gourmet restaurant in the new sprawling outdoor mall of Delsol, Arizona, a couple have just finished eating and remain sitting at their booth. Dr Jason Patane, a well-known surgeon, empties the last of the bottle of Chateau Blanc in his glass.

"Did you like the way I did it last night? Like a lollipop," asks his young companion flashing a coquettish smile.

"Hush." Weary of being seen in public with a teenage girl that could be his daughter, he checks around the dining hall for over-hearers.

"I learned at Horny Goat Pass."

"Horny what?"

"Horny Goat Pass, that place outside town."

"Never heard of it," he says still looking around. He appears nervous, pale, uneasy.

"The place where young people meet."

"Where's that?"

"All kids know about it, the canyon in the sand dunes."

"Didn't know there was such a place."

"South of town. Where they hold slumber parties." Her glowing face flashes her pearly teeth.

"Parties. What do you do there?"

"Kids bring in pot, booze and sex CD's. They drink till turning shitfaced, then, parking in rows, listen to rap music and do drugs and backseat sex."

"How did you learn so much about the subject?"

"Subject?"

"Sex," he says into her ear.

"Sex-Ed school. They teach us how not to get pregnant and give us condoms and pills. Me and my friends don't use condoms and pills but know how not to get pregnant."

"And so, you outsmart everybody."

"Sure do."

"How long have you been attending those parties?"

"Since I was fourteen…Amazing, I've bumped into the kids of policemen, teachers, businessmen, the mayor. One day I bumped into Marla, the preacher's daughter."

Noticing his uneasiness, she asks, "Are you afraid of being seen with me?"

"Is not that, Lolita. Some people love gossip. You look awfully young next to me."

"I'm not awfully young. I'm eighteen."

"Do you parents know?"

"Know what?"

"The slumber parties."

"Never suspected. We were good liars. I used to tell Mom I'd spend the weekend at my friend Mona's. Her parents traveled a lot and we often had the house for ourselves. Her little sis covered for us when Mom called to check on me. Ha, ha, ha." She flashes a smile. "While Mom slept the angels' dream, we were orgying."

"Remarkable!" He feels his chin dropping.

"Yes. The parties lasted all night and broke up at dawn. No chaperons but the moon, the stars and the crickets. Sunday nights, all cleaned up and made up, we returned home to prepare for Monday school."

She changes gears.

"Now, tell me about your first time," she says, observing him.

"My first time?"

"Yeah."

"You mean?"

"Right, I mean sex."

"Okay, but don't laugh."

"I promise not to," she says, wrinkling her eyebrows.

"I'm actually an introvert…

"My first time was when I got married to my high school sweetheart, my first love. I was twenty-eight."

73

She blocks a grin with her hand.

"See, I told you," he says.

"I'm sorry. Not making fun of you, I swear. Just felt like laughing."

Looking into her soda glass, "Tell me the truth about last night. Was I good?" she asks.

"You left me speechless."

"You mean you didn't like it?" He looks back at him.

"On the contrary! You were fabulous but let's change the subject, will you?" Nervous, he rotates his wine glass.

"Let me have some." She leans over and sips from his glass.

"Arg," she grimaces and wipes her thick red lips with the napkin. "It's gross."

"Yeah, it's rather dry."

His muscular arm wraps around her blond hair locks and neck.

"You're ice cold! Want your coat on?"

"No, I feel great."

He pulls her in and kisses her softly on the mouth, then sits back.

"How do you like the assistant-nurse's job?" he asks.

"Love it, except the old head-nurse, she's nasty."

"Nora? She's worked at the hospital since... before you were born."

"I think she should retire." She knits her eyebrows. "Ha, ha, ha," she smiles softly.

"What is it?"

"That little old lady's so funny, Ursula," Lolita evokes. "You ask 'How are you?' she answers, "Eighty three." You ask 'What's your name?' she says, 'Portland, Oregon.'" Lolita's humor is contagious.

"Ha, ha, ha, Mrs Parker? She suffers from Alzheimer's."

"And the other lady, Thelma. She calls me each time I walk by. 'Come sit here with me child,' she says. That's when I get in trouble. Nora hates us to fraternize."

Doctor Patane looks ahead vacantly. Cellular phone rings bring him back.

"In fifteen minutes? I'll hurry back."

He puts the phone back in his pocket. "Nurse Thelma reminding me I've surgery shortly."

He looks down, pensively.

"Penny for your thoughts," she says.

"You still love him, don't you?"

"Love him?"

"Nestor."

"Nestor! Ha, ha, ha. No, no, it's not love."

"What is it then? You used to hang on to him"

"Dunno what it was. It just happened. I get a job at his accounting office. My senior year, I need money for my prom dress and stuff. Then he starts chasing me all over the place. A ten-arm octopus! Wouldn't leave me in peace."

His gaze travels up the marble swellings under her low cut neck and stops at her hazel eyes.

"You're a splendorous work of art, a statue, the female of the species in her prime."

"What?"

"I said what I said."

"You crazy nut, ha, ha, ha."

"Don't mind me. Just a reverie."

"Anyway, he says he's crazy about me. To prove it, the jerk leaves his wife and asks me to marry him. Ha, ha, ha, I crack up. 'Marry you? You must be nuts!' He doesn't let down. I go along 'cause I like the presents he gives me and driving his Jaguar convertible."

"But you had his child."

"I didn't mean to. One of those things. He kept yanking off his rubber. We didn't know whose baby till he had the test done."

"DNA."

"Ahem. When my mom found out, she made a big scene and wouldn't let me get rid of it."

"It wouldn't've been nice"

"Look, he's not for me. I'm eighteen. Just out of high school. He's forty-five. A dirty old fart. With that gray squirrel-tail beard over his face, he looks old. Besides, he hates dance and doesn't dig my friends."

He appears defensive.

"I'm not too young myself. Thirty-five next month, could be your father."

"My father?"

"I mean, you look fifteen. My colleagues call me a cradle raider."

She examines him. "You're handsome, Jason. Many of my friends envy your chiseled body." She squeezes his solid bicep.

"When's the last time you were with him?" he says, concerned.

"A few days ago, before we met. He was becoming a pest. Fighting all the time. One day he pushed me against the wall when I'd come back from a night out… after he'd given me permission!"

"Have you told him about us?"

"Yesterday. He threw a fit. Hit the wall so hard he broke his knuckles. Then, the crazy jerk pulled a knife out of a kitchen drawer and threatened to stick it in his heart. He's such a bozo."

"He seems unstable. Be careful. Do you have to meet him again?"

"He's harmless. I know him. Anyway, I've walked out on him. Told him over the phone I wouldn't be back, and again today when he called to apologize."

He gulps down the wine and waves to the waiter.

"We've got to leave. I'll be late for surgery. That's the problem with being a surgeon and the reason why my wife and I became distant, no private life. Where's our waiter… There he is!"

He waves his arm vigorously, but the waiter, a tray in hand, sweeps by ignoring him.

"What the h-, as if we were invisible." He waves to other waiters, waitresses, nobody listens.

"We've been abandoned. This is rude."

"It's crowded. They must be real busy," she observes.

"But those people at the next table came on later, have eaten, paid, and left already. It's remarkable."

"Why don't we just walk out of here? My friend Lisa and I did it once. Nobody paid attention and we had a free meal. It was a riot!"

"We might just do that."

Suddenly, a surge of excitement, a nervous trepidation overtakes the morose restaurant personnel.

Irrelevant whispers, mumbles and aimless pacing replace the various tasks of the food serving business.

Under the indirect lighting, the subdued atmosphere of the restaurant turns frantic. The waiters desert their posts, put down trays, water and coffee pitchers, and run toward the foyer.

Patrons at their tables stop the dining and drinking and intrigued, crane their necks in the direction of the commotion.

A girl, fear-flushed face on, stomps in from the parking lot. "Someone got shot! Someone got shot! Out in the parking lot!"

Diners abandon their tables and dash toward the front entrance—a rout en masse.

"I'm going out. You better stay here," Jason says, pushing the table away.

"No! I'm going out with you," she says, shadowing him. He catches up with two weepy waitresses.

"Who got shot?" Jason asks, but they ignore him hands over their gaping mouths.

Holding hands, the doctor and Lolita step outside. It's dark beyond the entrance and the crowds block the view from the parking lot.

"Who got shot? Who got shot? I'm a doctor. I'm a doctor!" he yells.

Men, women, and restaurant personnel are so absorbed in the incident that they don't even turn their heads to heed the doctor's words. He overhears a couple ahead of him. He cranes his neck between them and listens.

"I saw the whole thing," the man tells his female companion. "The couple walked out of the restaurant and were approaching their car when a man came out of the shadows, gun in hand, sneaked up on 'em from the back, and shot 'em both in the head without saying a word. Bam, bam, execution-style. They dropped dead and he ran back into the darkness where he'd come from."

"You take a good look at him?" his companion asks.

"Not very good, just a shadow."

Jason and Lolita sneak around the couple.

"I'm a doctor. I'm a doctor."

They slip through the throngs of the curious to approach the focus of the commotion. It comes from the area where the doctor's car is parked.

They push their way through and finally reach ground zero, the zone of the incident.

"I'm a doctor!"

Jason steps up next to the circle of people standing around or crouching down by the stricken couple.

77

Victims are lying supine next to the doctor's car, the car door open, keys on the lock. They're not moving. White handkerchiefs cover their faces. Blood spreads out around their heads like crimson halos over the pavement.

"I'm a doctor."

Jason, Lolita beside him, kneels down as someone pulls the handkerchiefs away form the victims' faces. Shell-shocked he collapses backwards on the asphalt.

"O my god, it's…it's…"

"IT'S US!" horrified, she screams through her fingers.

6. MONA LISA

Detective Reynolds arrived a few minutes after the CSI team. The first blues at the scene had cordoned off a house located in the old section of Delsol, Arizona.

A mature lady lay supine on the living room floor, nude from the waist down, skirt lifted over her face.

The driver of the Lunch-On-Wheels van discovered the body. "I-I felt her pulse for signs of life. The smell of acid made me dizzy," the old man said, faltering. "I-I ran to the bathroom, got sick, and called 911."

A bottle of Drano lay empty nearby. The acid had been poured over her abdomen and had faded or eaten away the floor carpet around the body.

"She's in the height of rigor mortis, twelve or so hours from time of death, corroborated by the rectal temperature," said the assistant coroner.

The scene revealed innumerable half-velocity blood smears and splatters. Searching for eyewitnesses, the detective found a half-conscious transient spread-eagled in a nearby alley behind a trash dumpster. He'd seen a husky woman hurrying away from the victim's house the night before.

"Sh-she almost tripped on me, b-but didn't notice my presence," he said.

Reynolds doubted his testimony would be of any help. Defense counsel shows no mercy with intoxicated witnesses. Suspects had been arrested, jailed, indicted, tried, and then freed because of unreliable eyewitness reports.

Miss Ruth McCoy could have been anybody's mother figure: vivacious, intelligent, a retired grammar school teacher, never married, dedicated to education. She wrote poetry, spoke languages and liked to read. Her ex-students acclaimed and respected her.

"At 68, my doctor told me to stop worrying about my health. That my organs were fit and full of energy, like an adolescent's," she said with braggadocio.

Close to the railroad station, across from an ancient hotel that had been the lodging of Clark Gable and John Wayne while shooting Westerns, she lived in a house located in the Old Town area. Built in the 1920s and declared a historical landmark, it was still full of style and ancient luxury.

It featured wooden floors, vaulted ceilings, rounded corners, spacious bedrooms, and large baths with original fixtures. Timely maintenance and TLC had kept all functioning.

Friends and relatives warned her more than once that the old town section, now drastically changed, was an unsafe place for a single lady, and urged her to move to a safer area. Adamantly, Ruth refused to leave her lodgings. Not rich and keeping no valuables at home, she feared no evil. She'd given most of her assets away and relied on her pension check.

"Bait for thieves? Not likely. Besides, I want to die here where I was born," she told them, with that benevolent smile that never abandoned her.

*　*　*

Learning of Ms McCoy's murder, Det Joe Maravilla, of Homicide, asked the captain to exempt him from the case because he was so personally involved. His pain was unbearable. When he met her, she was a successful organizer of funding drives to benefit families of officers killed in the line of duty. Since then, she had become close to him and his family. Lately, the friendship had cooled down and reunions had become more sporadic. Not of her doing though, he had become more immersed in cold homicide cases and less outgoing.

"Mother-less since my infant years, I considered her my second mom. That was ten years ago, and I always kept a place in my heart for that kind woman," Maravilla muttered.

After twenty years in the Department, Maravilla was nearing his retirement date.

His bored wife had run away with a rich cattleman, but he hardly noticed the difference as he had turned into a workaholic.

His daughter Norma, twenty, lived in California. They kept in touch. He dreamt of having her join him upon his retirement. And with that in mind, he'd bought a cozy two-bedroom home in a quiet area of Del Norte.

"We're family and shouldn't live apart, don't you think so?" he called her up after his divorce, but she avoided the issue.

"Thank you papa, but I'm happy living on my own, and would rather stay like this." End of call.

Det Reynolds took over the original investigation without any luck. Days passed, weeks, two years, and Reynolds transferred to another jurisdiction. The case languished in the Delsol PD's basement storage. Then, one day, when the pain ameliorated, Maravilla decided to take a fresh look at the cold case.

He re-examined McCoy's dossier and found that all blood spatters at the crime scene belonged to the victim. There was no new evidence. Killer had left neither clues nor bodily fluids and had carefully wiped off all prints.

Descending the steps down the Evidence Property Room to put the borrowed file back, a light lit in his mind. The report mentioned a witness—someone by the name of Tom Rex.

Maravilla contacted the DMV, the welfare office, the Social Security Administration. He hit pay dirt at the Old Mission. One of the hobos told him where to find him. Rex had moved to Los Angeles.

Maravilla took the next plane to LA. He brought along his department's profile artist. They found the wino sitting on the sidewalk catching the warm rays of the morning sun outside a Main St mission, downtown.

Spirits had turned his nose the color of The Red Nose Dear. A bottle of fine Scotch sharpened his recollections better than any memory potion. He gave them a talking picture of the woman running away from the crime scene. His sharp image of the suspect was remarkable coming from someone with such a gaunt appearance.

With the precious artist's drawing in their possession, the lawmen boarded the next flight back to Delsol. Aboard the plane, Maravilla had a brain flash.

His years in the force had sharpened his powers of observation. He recognized in the drawing of the husky woman the face of Lazar Morpheus, alias Mona Lisa, a registered sex offender with a long record; a former inmate of infamous Hellhole Prison. Back at HQ, he went back downstairs and plunked out the suspect's records and spirited them out to his home for a closer examination. Its pages contained a detailed scenario of Morpheus's crimes and Maravilla immersed himself in the read.

Morpheus' troubles with the law started two decades back. His wife ran a child care business. She was the sole breadwinner since he refused to hold any honorable job. In exchange, he pretended to be her assistant. In her absence, he raped several children entrusted to their care and taped the episodes; then, sold the videos to pedophiles through an Internet site.

The police followed the computer trail and learned his name and address. Detectives communicated confidentially their findings to his wife. After learning he might have raped his own, she consented to secretly videotaping him while alone with the children. The detectives jumped on him from the closet and cuffed him attempting to rape another child.

Searching his garage they found a wealth of evidence, incriminating videos cassettes, sound tapes and photographs. Some videos showed him with his own offspring. It was enough proof to indict, convict, and sentence him to thirty years in prison.

He was locked up in a federal center for the rehabilitation of offenders serving time with antecedents of bestiality, necrophilia, sadomasochism, pedophilia, fetishism and rape. The news of his deeds spread out among the inmates and more than one looked forward to spending a good time with him. When his incarceration began, he stumbled in leg shackles donning pink prison fashions, past rows of iron cages, populated with a menagerie of stalking blood-shot eyes and salivating mouths agonizing behind bars. He heard a few scream, "Honey!"

Some years later a national TV network doing a documentary on sex offender rehabilitation recorded his interview. The documentary backfired. Far from being rehabilitated, he bragged about his exploits and that incarceration, rather than punishment, had been a pleasure trip. Because of prison overcrowding and good behavior, he was let out in twenty years.

His wife had divorced him long before and changed her and their children's surnames. He'd been paroled prior to the old teacher's murder and presumably gone good. He'd kept clean since then and his parole officer had no complaints. Morpheus supported himself with odd menial jobs and a welfare check. He lived alone and had kept clean, or so it seemed. Maravilla finished reading, and wrote down an address on his notebook.

He arrived at Morpheus's pad, an ancient motel in the historical downtown section converted into low-income rentals. He knocked. Through the two-inch slit of the door, a pair of fish-cold, blood-shot eyes flickered on top of a mysterious Mona Lisa-esque smile. The lips were thin, the line of the mouth straight and arching slightly at the ends. A smile like no other. A permanent feature. A diabolical straight line, cold, sardonic. Maravilla pulled out his badge.

"Can I come in?"

Morpheus opened the door wider and both stood face-to-face on the threshold.

"What's the cops doin' here, may I ask? I've kept clean. A model citizen, just ask my parole officer," Morpheus said in a fastidious, shrilly voice, like a ventriloquist, through the imperceptible lip split.

"I know that," said Maravilla. "The purpose of my visit, I need your help. You're a smart man. Streetwise. You can help me solve an old murder case."

There was no reaction. The Mona Lisa grin remained like a groove etched permanently on stone.

"Remember Ruth McCoy? That old lady murdered a block from here?"

"Am I supposed to know her? I don't even know my next-door neighbors. Who was she?"

"The 68-year-old retired school teacher. It made the headlines. The attack happened two years ago today."

"McCoy, McCoy, it rings a bell. Oh yeah, this is a small town, crimes like that are big news."

"We've no clues but we think the killer hasn't left the area. You've been around here since about the time of the crime and have met a lot of people, you know, locals and transplants coming and going. Most surely, the killer's still among us." And he stressed this.

"I think you can help us solve this case…

"There's a reward for information leading to an arrest. Why don't you come down to police HQ tomorrow and help us out?"

"I'm not sure I can be of any help. But I'll think it over."

"Come down anyway. I know you're on the good side of the law now. That's why I'm knocking on your door."

Maravilla stepped back out and handed him a business card. For days, Maravilla waited in vain for a word from Morpheus. A week later he repeated the visit to the suspect and re-issued the invitation to HQ. This time Morpheus called first and showed up next morning.

It was almost impossible to prove Morpheus had been the killer. The authorities did not have a shred of evidence, forensic or otherwise, to connect him to the killing. They had an eyewitness, but his memories were of dubious value coming from the marinated brain of a wino in the last stages of liver cirrhosis.

They sat across a table in an interrogation room disguised as a cozy den. A large seascape picture hung on a wall. Really a two-way mirror. Det Nolan, Homicide, and another detective peeked in on the interview across the glass. Morpheus looked around, crossed his legs, leaned back, and made himself comfortable.

Maravilla pulled a pile of photos from a dossier labeled McCoy and spread them out on the table like a Chinese paper fan.

When Morpheus saw the photos of the murdered woman, he kept a poker face under the perennial and unchangeable grin. Yet, Maravilla had learnt to detect the minutest changes in demeanor during his twenty years in Homicide. The detective noticed a slight tensing up of the neck cords, imperceptible to the untrained eye.

Convinced he'd found McCoy's killer, poker-faced himself, he didn't give out a hint of his suspicions. He perceived the one across the table as the shrewdest of criminals and that this would turn out to be a titanic battle of wits. Morpheus kept denying he'd ever met or seen the victim.

"Poor old woman. This was the job of a monster. A drug-crazed jerk. Can't think of anyone now but I'll ask around," said Morpheus, his words coming through a slight parting of the lips.

"Call if a name comes up, will ya?" asked Maravilla.

Maravilla spent a few more minutes with this person of interest. He realized he'd reached a dead end. Morpheus was not going to incriminate himself. He asked him if he would submit to a lie detector test.

"I am not ready now. Maybe in the future, though I got nothing to hide," he answered.

Maravilla had no probable cause and Morpheus had the right to refuse the test. Evidence against him just did not exist. Both knew that.

Maravilla replaced the photos and wrapped the dossier with the rubber band. He placed it on the side of the table. He asked Morpheus to wait a few more minutes. Morpheus was getting uncomfortable and it didn't escape Maravilla's notice.

"Mr Morpheus, before you leave, Det Nolan'd like to have a word with you. You don't mind?"

"I do mind, Maravilla. Got better things to do than waste my time with ya. Better make it snappy."

Nolan walked in as Maravilla disappeared through the side door. He found Morpheus resting his arms on the table, uneasy, fighting imaginary ants off his fingers. The detective balanced his arse at the end of the interrogator's chair.

"I'm Nolan. Det Maravilla's told me of your offer to help us in the investigation on the murder of Ruth McCoy."

 "Told Maravilla I know nothing about it. Ain't saying another word. Period."

"I know. That's why I'm here. Did he read you your Miranda rights yet?"

"No, did he need to? I'm not a suspect."

"I know. And what did you tell him about a lawyer for you?"

"I say an innocent man don't need one," Morpheus said, his obfuscation mounting.

"I think you do. We know you're a fucking liar and a murderer," Nolan said, pushing back against his chair, banging his fat fist on the table and stabbing him with irate eyes.

There is an unbearable pause.

The Mona Lisa line purses with suppressed fury. Morpheus' face drains of color.

"I want to see your face in front of all these pictures…"
Nolan adds, unwrapping the folder and throwing the photos on the table.

With a swing of his hand, like bowling pins, Morpheus tosses the photos to the floor.

"You've got nothin' on me. This shit interview's over!"

Morpheus springs up to his feet. "You can't stop me. Good bye pig!" he yelps, storming out the door.

Maravilla and fellow detectives see him stomp down the hall, the fish catch that got away. They join Nolan on the other side of the mirror. Words aren't necessary; tense silence says it all.

Others did, but Maravilla never gave up. Months passed and Morpheus was almost forgotten at the PD.

But Maravilla, one excuse or another, kept in touch with the suspect. He visited Morpheus at his apartment and even apologized for Nolan's rudeness. He kind of succeeded keeping a tenuous line of communication open. Maravilla managed to make a good impression on the suspect.

Maravilla knew this area. He used to cruise it often while on patrol. It hadn't changed. A few blocks from the railroad station, the streets shut down at dusk. The few pedestrians, lone transients fumigated by an excess of liquor or drugs.

The scarce cars trudging the streets cruise with care and windows locked, as are businesses and residences' doors after dusk. The Old Mission and two other flophouses for the homeless stand near the tracks. Delsol, AZ, is a convenient stop for train hoppers and hobos heading for the big cities.

There was someone in the Department who empathized with Maravilla's quest, Tony Rico, an undercover from Vice. They had a chat once over lunch at Jumbo Subs. Rico was in his thirties but prematurely aged, gaunt and hippy-like with a long graying beard and unkempt yellow shoulder-length hair. He sat across the dinner table. Both lawmen showed the facial marks of the war of attrition against crime.

"Remember the unsolved case of Ruth McCoy, the retired school teacher found raped and strangled in his living room?" Maravilla opened.

"Yes, that was over two years ago. What ever happened? Found any leads yet?"

"Reynolds handled that case. The few clues led nowhere. Looked like a random crime. Reynolds transferred to California and they sent the folder to the cold files."

"What about Forensics?"

"This is a small town. We've got last priority. If you're a murderer, do it in a small town. Chances are you won't get caught."

"I remember. It happened near the tracks. It had to be a transient's job," recalled Rico.

"I went through the file the other day and found an eyewitness. A derelict slumbering in an alley across McCoy's house had a good description of the killer. We located the old man in LA and he gave us a good description."

"Someone we know?"

"Yeah. It fits a local guy. One by the name of Lazar Morpheus. Served time for child molesting. Still lives in town registered as a class-3 sex offender. I've interviewed him but couldn't get anything out of him. His alibi's shaky but there's nothing to connect him. Forensics couldn't find a thing."

"What about the eyewitness?"

"Oh man, a wino in the last stages of liver collapse. The defense would tear him apart; that what he saw was an episode of delirium tremens. You know how it is, we stand no chance in court with what we've got. The only hope's a confession. But he's too smart. He suspects we're after him and knows we've got nothing. Thinks he got away with murder—the perfect crime."

Maravilla sits back reading something in Rico's eyes. He preempts him.

"I thought about it. Put a contract on him? I wouldn't dare. Couldn't go that road. We're here to enforce the law, not break it."

They shared their love for Ms McCoy and their hate for the murderer.

"I can't forget Ms McCoy, my grammar teacher. She treated us like her own—a second mother to us all. I went to her funeral and cried like a child. One of the few times I ever did," said Rico, eyes moist. Unable to keep on eating, he tossed the uneaten submarine in the next trash basket and spitted out the bite of sandwich.

As Rico recalled Ms McCoy's murder and its lurid details his pain turned to rage. Indignation mounted and both detectives found it hard to contain their bile against the homicidal maniac. Then, they broke up the chat and went back to their respective duty stations.

Next day Maravilla's phone rang. It was Rico, excited.

"Got an idea to catch a murderer. Didn't sleep last night thinking about it."

He'd entice Morpheus to make a faux pas fabricating a story about a local doctor who'd passed away of a stroke two years ago.

He hoped Morpheus would take the bait. The idea was to smear the reputation of the late old woman and give the impression that her assassin had done a great service to society. A risky and unorthodox, in police annals, course of action. If discovered by Internal Affairs, the conspirators could kiss their careers good bye.

For their plan, they needed assistance inside the PD's records office and they got it from a clerk in the Department. A middle-aged woman who'd been Maravilla's lover before he was afflicted with erectile dysfunction. Using department forms, stationary and seals, she fabricated a file reclassifying the natural death of the doctor to death at the hands of another. Purportedly, the corpse had been exhumed and re-examined, and poison found in the tissues. And more importantly, a suspect's name came up, Ruth McCoy.

Thus prepared, Maravilla paid Morpheus one more visit and invited him to the Red Cage bar. They sat at a corner table and Maravilla touched the subject of Ruth McCoy. Morpheus's shifting eyes insinuated his delight at the extra attention bestowed on him. He was starting to feel fondness for the detective. After a few minutes of meaningless chat and two draft beers, Maravilla pulled out a bunch of old paper cutouts from the local newspaper. Then he read from the fake police report dated a few days prior to McCoy's death.

After Morpheus had had a cursory look over the clippings and paperwork, Maravilla said casually: "You know, I shouldn't talk about the dead like that but the little old lady was no saint. Under a clean and honorable patina, she hid a sordid second life. Her reputation was crumbling down. Ancient crimes were finally catching up with her. Evidence emerged of child sex abuse and drug dealings during her teaching school days. But there's more. She might have been a murderess as well."

He spread out the old and faded obituary of the passing away of Dr Pillborough. "An arrest warrant had been issued on the poisoning of doctor Pillborough," Maravilla continued. "Forensics finally caught up with her two years ago. Dr Pillborough was the first one who confronted her with allegations from one of her former students about the child abuse episodes. Big mistake not going straight to the police! She killed him with cyanide-laced cookies. Nobody suspected foul play. The ME zeroed in on an aneurysm as cause of death and closed the case…

"There was no reason to suspect otherwise. The good doctor had no enemies. But then, a neighbor's complain triggered an investigation. Her pets had been poisoned. A police-installed camera taped McCoy red-handedly baiting another neighbor's cat and dog.

"Dr Pillborough's case was re-opened. His exhumed body showed traces of cyanide. The judge issued an arrest warrant but someone got ahead and did her in saving the taxpayers a lot of money."

Maravilla finished his cigarette and screwed the glowing filter in the ashtray.

"I knew she was a bitch," Morpheus murmured silently between teeth. It was imperceptible but Maravilla could clearly read the lip movements. *He just declared he knew her*, he thought without giving a hint. *We need a confession now.*

Maravilla came back wired, but nothing that Morpheus said—he said nothing relevant anyway—would incriminate him. For the rest of the chat, Morpheus used extra caution. Maravilla couldn't break the barrier. Morpheus resulted wittier than his stalkers. Discouraged, Maravilla regretfully got ready to send McCoy's folder back downstairs for good. Next day he met the anxious Rico at Jumbo's.

"How did it go," asked Rico.

"No luck. He suspects. He'll never confess, I know."

They ate in silence. Rico stopped in the middle of his sandwich, swallowing hard.

"I had another brainstorm," Rico said. "Look, I'm undercover now. Nobody in the street knows me. We plant something on him. Notify his parole officer. Lock him up for a few days. I get picked up for a bogus charge and locked up with him. His own cellmate. I gain his confidence. I'm wired. I get the confession."

"That's very farfetched. Are you sure you'd do that?"

"I'm willing to try anything. Closure for me is seeing his ass executed."

"I won't retire in peace till that happens."

"We've gotta go to work and get the DA on our side," Rico said.

"We won't mention the planted evidence though."

The detectives twisted the law slightly. After all, the victim clamored for justice. Carl Carlton, the county district attorney, heard Maravilla. Carlton didn't say much, but after recalling the old murder, his nostrils flared. Carlton met with Rico.

"Okay Tony Rico, we're going to put your plan into action. We'll indict you for something serious, have you picked up, and locked up for a while. You sure you want to go ahead with this?"

Two blues found Morpheus at midnight dressed in drag outside the Red Cage bar.

"You can't arrest me. The government's not gonna tell me how to dress."

"I'm arresting you for prostitution and theft," one officer said. "We've got a complaint and a witness."

"Well, kiss my sweet ass. I'm gonna sue all of you bastards. First, I want a lawyer."

"You'll call him in the morning. Tonight, you'll spend the night in the cage."

Morpheus demanded a public defender and respect for his constitutional rights. The night judge showed signs of exasperation when he set bail of $10,000. He had to let him go soon unless the officer had more evidence. This one showed the judge the statement from the witness. A guy said he picked the suspect up downtown mistaking him for a girl. He paid the fee for sex and they went to a motel. There, he discovered the gender ruse and angrily protested followed by Morpheus storming out of the room. He noticed his wallet missing. He had $4,000 in it. Something like that is what he put on paper and signed it. The officers testified they found the wallet and the money in Morpheus's possession.

This was grand theft and a serious parole violation. The judge reluctantly agreed to raise the bail to $50,000, cash only, a figure Morpheus could never afford. Further, the judge ordered him locked up till the bail was paid. Two detention officers dragged Morpheus out the courtroom and into a holding cell.

Next day, the jailers escorted Rico to Morpheus's cell. This one looked at him with curiosity as they locked and slammed the door behind the undercover. The cell was neat. Morpheus was a good housekeeper. Rico put his toothbrush and personals on the vacant upper bunk, clambered up and went to sleep. He was awakened by the dinner call. The cellmates got their dinner trays through the bars and ate in silence. Morpheus stared.

"Stop looking at me with that stupid smile. Don't you have another face?" Rico asked.

"Don't have to be so nasty…

"After all, we're gonna share this cell for a while," Morpheus answered, grinning.

"Just stay away from me. You're repugnant."

Morpheus acted nonchalantly first, completely normal. During the night, he made the first advance. He approached him. Rico recoiled.

"Look, keep your distance. I don't do that shit. Stay away from me or I'll break your ass."

It worked. Morpheus returned docilely to his bunker and did not insist that night. Next morning, he started a conversation.

"Why are you in for?"

"I fell in love with an underage girl," said Rico.

"I know all about it. I did time for loving kids. And it almost ruined my life. I spent twenty years in the slammer."

"I know what you mean. I served time for that too."

And that ended their introduction. Two days lapsed. Not a word was spoken between the cellmates. The lights went off the third night. The inmates retired to their bunks to do their things—read, write, sleep, whatever.

Early morning Rico felt a hand around his crutch. Morpheus grabbed his rod and put it in his mouth. Rico twisted with rage and boiled over. He was about to jump up and beat Morpheus to a pulp but the memory of the old teacher kept him silent.

Fellatio was repeated the next and the next morning. During the day Morpheus professed his love for the detective.

That time Rico mentioned the McCoy murder but Morpheus ignored him. Further hints about the unsolved case elicited no reactions. He surmised he had brought up the matter of the crime too soon. He decided to beat around the bushes for a while.

After hours of unsubstantial chat, the opportunity arose. Facing each other at opposite ends of the cell, Morpheus wanted to know what Rico was in for.

"I'm a high school teacher. She acted and looked much older than her real fourteen. I couldn't resist. She was beautiful and I like underage girls. I fell for her like an idiot. I did no harm—gave her all my love."

Rico started crying. "Why, why, why?" And he went on with his charade in this manner. He was an excellent actor and Morpheus seemed to sympathize with his ordeal.

"Now, I gotta face the consequences. We live in a goddamned puritan society. She cried when I was arrested. She loved me. Now, I don't know. Guess they'll turn her against me. Her parents and the school want blood and I'm the sacrificial goat." Facing away, he waited for Morpheus's reaction.

"What about you, Lazar?" he asked.

"My troubles started long ago. I liked much younger stuff—a penchant for toddlers. My ex-wife ran a childcare business. I didn't give a shit if I got caught. When I saw a child I gasped for air. They threw the book at me. Thirty years. Every single day in prison I thought of taking revenge on puritan society. I kept the flame of hate alive those long days in my cell imagining the shittiest things I could do after my release. And I did a lot of shit. But the one I'm proudest of is the number on that old hag McCoy, he, he, he."

"McCoy? Ruth McCoy?"

"The same."

"And how did you do it, ha, ha, ha. Tell me. I'm all ears."

And Morpheus said, pacing back and forth in the cell:

"Restless that morning 'cause my lover was messin' around with several men and women—shit, some people don't care about feelings and his fuckin' attitude made me furious... I gulped down some pills, whisky, and had a few blows of meth. I dressed in drag and walked out. I recalled the old lady at the end of the street, so I looked around. Nobody'd seen me. I stopped by her house, jumped the fence, and peeped in through the window.

"I caught sight of her ass pouring a can of Campbell soup into boiling water. I knocked. WHO IS IT? I knocked. WHO IS IT? Then, she came up to the door askin' again. I answered in my sweetest lingo, Ma'am, your next-door neighbor, if you need your yard swept or any type of work around the house. Government check hasn't come in yet. Willin' to work for food.

"Oh, oh, you have to do nothing; I'll give you five dollars, nice, young woman. She opened the door a bit but left the chain on. As she dug in her purse for change, I kicked the door in and jumped on her. I hit her hard with fist and foot and dragged her by the hair to the couch where I socked her with a few more pops. Oh, she fought back like a lioness and dashed to the kitchen, me in chase. Shit, the old bitch burned my face with hot soup and tried to pull my eyes."

Morpheus became agitated. His neck cords stuck out.

Tears misted his eyes.

"Fuck, she had no right to cause me so much harm. It made me MAD, MAD, MAD! I slapped her many times till she got stunned. Grabbed a screen cord and tied her hands down but she kept screaming and calling me offensive names that hurt, PERVERT, IDIOT, MONSTER. I ripped her pants off and raped her. Shit, her body was feeble and spent by the ravages of age and she'd lived well beyond her prime.

"Fuck, she wouldn't stop callin' me ANIMAL and my fury blew up. I suffocated her with a pillow and finished her off with my hands. Hell, she hardly resisted. She gave a few kicks of joy at my lovemaking. Sure she enjoyed like a cow.

"I ransacked the house for valuables and found a small amount of cash hidden in the pantry and some jewelry, mostly worthless K-Mart shit. I pulled a gallon of Drano from under the sink and poured it down her vagina to kill the evidence. Shit, I know acid destroys evidence and sends frustrated coroners and prosecutors crawling up the walls."

"D-did you ever feel regret?" asked Rico, nauseated, after a pause.

"Shit, you kiddin'? She was old and spent—a mean old hag and a murderer. Oh, I'm still young. It's the law of nature. Dunno why all the fuzz."

Rico, crying like a baby, took a feline leap across the cell. With adrenalin-multiplied strength he grabbed Morpheus and tried to snap his neck. But then, Maravilla and two guards entered the cell and yanked Rico back from his prey and held him down with a massive effort.

"Settle down Rico. We've got him on tape!" exclaimed Maravilla. Rico composed himself, yanked the taped hidden microphone from his chest and handed it to Maravilla.

Some time later Morpheus sat puzzled in his cell. Something dawned on him that he'd been taken for a ride.

An hour later, Maravilla and Rico arrived at the DA's office. They placed the incriminating tape on his desk. Rico felt sick and excused himself, went to the bathroom and vomited for half an hour. After debriefing at the PD, Rico boarded an ambulance for his trip to the psychiatric ward of the Delsol Medical Center.

"Doubt I can keep sane any longer…

"I'm past due for intensive care, and a long vacation," he told the paramedic.

Four weeks later, his beard shaved off, hair trimmed, donning clean civvies, he arrived at his house anxious to see wife and kids. They weren't home. He found a note on the kitchen table.

"Tony, you have changed a lot. I've learned about your pervert habits. Your job's more important than your wife and kids. We've left you. Don't try to approach us. I'm filing for divorce. Sorry. Jan."

Tony closed his tear-soaked eyes. "There must've been a leak at the Department."

When all legal maneuvers, including entrapment, failed, Morpheus through his public defender asked for a plea agreement in exchange for his life, but the DA held firm like a wall.

All quarters wanted him dead.

Convicted, the jury asked for the death sentence and the judge granted it.

A few years later, the lines on his face showing the tortuous prison ways, the IV poisons rendered him lifeless. Yet, even after death, the Mona Lisa smile didn't abandon him even as his carcass disappeared behind the metal trap of the fiery cremation chamber.

7. THE REST STOP MURDERS

The early morning twilight carpeted Interstate-8 turning the ghostly night denizens into real trees, rocks and hills before his eyes. Approaching the Arizona-California state line just west of Gallina, AZ, and groggy from his long, solo stretch of driving, Joe Maravilla drank up the last of his thermo coffee.

He pulled off the road at a highway rest area. He alighted and stretched his legs. Walking to the restroom, he passed a black Mercedes. He found the tinted windows intact but cracked as if they had gone through a rollover.

"Strange sight," he muttered, "yet, I have a long trip ahead and this is none of my business."

He climbed in his van, buckled up and switched on. A sudden concern gnawed at his entrails, a common feeling in the lawmen community. He switched off, unbuckled and inched back to the black car. Circling and craning his head up and down ostrich-like, he tried to peek into the interior through the murky glass.

93

Two young men on their way back from the restrooms stopped and stood silently behind him.

"Is this your vehicle?" Maravilla asked, startled by two shadows cast against the car.

"Course not, we're ridin' the Bronco," one said, pointing to their car. "Anything wrong?"

By the front end, Maravilla leaned over the tinted windshield glass and gazed in.

The sight of four fatalities in the front and back seats with bloody pulps where their faces should've been gave him a jolt of vertigo. He'd seen it before. The victims' faces had been blown off with a shotgun. Tempted to open the door, he decided not to. No kind of first aid could help someone well along rigor mortis. He ran back to his car, unfolded his cellular and dialed emergency. He returned as a number of onlookers with a smell for the weird and nose for the odd had gathered around the Mercedes.

"Stay back. I'm a cop," he lied, as this was his first day of retirement from the force. "It's a crime scene. Nobody touch anything. Back-up's on the way."

He proceeded to encircle the area with crime scene tape pulled from the trunk of his car. Ten minutes later, a Crown Victoria with a sheriff's logo arrived.

"I'd pulled into the rest stop at 0530 hrs. Back from the restroom, I approached that black Mercedes," he told the sheriff deputy and his lady back up as they bailed out of their cruiser.

"Through the windshield glass, I observed an adult WM slumped on the driver's seat and an adult WF on the passenger's. I saw a juvenile WM and a juvenile WF embracing, leaning against each other in the center of the back seat. All victims showed buckshot wounds to the face. I saw no signs of life. The shooting must've occurred hours before by the appearance of the dry splatter on the interior."

"Who are you?" she asked pulling out her notebook.

"Joe Maravilla," he said, flashing his badge. "Just retired from Delsol PD- Homicide."

She wrote, First Witness at the Scene, on top of the page. She asked for additional ID and he produced his driver's license while the male deputy rushed to the Mercedes.

"Any more witnesses?"

"I don't think so. Onlookers gathered later, but I'd protected the area with barricade tape. Didn't touch anything."

"Mr Maravilla, please stick around. The detectives might want to take down your declaration," she said.

The male deputy crossed the taped perimeter while she phoned for the investigating team; then, she retrieved a number of traffic cones from the cruiser's trunk and sealed the highway rest stop to incoming traffic.

The deputy sheriff slipped on his crime scene gloves and opened the unlocked driver's door. The driver, a middle-aged man, fell down on him like a chopped log. Startled and blood-smeared, the cop pushed him back against the seat but the man stubbornly swung in the opposite direction. He collapsed over the lap of a second corpse, a mature woman of similar age on the passenger seat.

Panning his eyes right, he discovered two faceless young people in the back seat. He remembered his CVR training. But never mind. Nobody could survive this type of wounds. *Dead as doornails*, he thought. Covering his nose, the small town deputy took final mental notes of the deceased. A dozen onlookers craned their necks over the perimeter tape.

"This butcher shop smell!" he complained, folding over and slamming the door.

Additional police and the SCI personnel arrived and spread out. Two blues cleared the area of civilians by encouraging motorists to resume their interrupted trips west. Detectives, investigators in protective gear, and photographers processed the occurrence. The assistant coroner wrote down the apparent cause of death, checked for rigor mortis, and measured temperatures for estimated time of death. Reporters in the local channel van recorded the incident for the television news. An hour later, medics loaded the bagged bodies and the ambulances pulled away without fanfare.

Joe Maravilla briefed his counterpart, Det Dobbs of the Gallina PD, regarding his macabre find, and showing signs of exhaustion asked to be excused from the area.

"Go ahead with your trip," Det Dobbs said, "but do keep in touch."

Maravilla nodded on the way to his car. Aboard, he quickly gained cruising speed and continued his voyage west, but nagging images of the crime scene flashed in his mind.

Trees, highway signs, cars and even motorists had stolen the grotesque faces, or non-faces, of the deceased. An hour later, he stopped on the shoulder of the road to wipe the wet off his forehead. After two minutes that felt much longer, he made a U turn at the next exit.

"The hell with my retirement. This crime's revolting. My duty as a citizen, if not an ex-cop, is helping snare and put away an unleashed vicious beast," he muttered.

Eastbound, he passed by the scene of the tragedy. The rest stop had forgotten and forgiven. The crime team had disbanded and a stream of motorists had resumed driving in and out oblivious to the recent blood bath.

The flat and straight-like-arrow line of the asphalt had a hypnotic effect. Maravilla strived to keep awake. Lone driving was not his favorite pastime.

* * *

Det Maravilla had worked 20 years in the Department, ten in Homicide. He'd sold his house in Delsol, AZ, and paid off his bills. He didn't want to hear about the crime subject for the rest of his days; yet, Fate would not grant him his wish.

Now divorced, he'd fathered a 21-year-old daughter. Ex-wife had run away with the milkman, the biggest milk producer in the area, Rich Kreamer of Kreamer Cattle Company. Now, he carried his most precious possessions in the trunk of his car. Ten manuscripts inspired by prominent homicides that had shaken the town during his stretch as detective at Delsol PD. He wanted to make scriptwriting his second career.

Heading for Hollywood, California, he planned to peddle his crime stories to movie moguls and, hopefully, get someone interested in taking them to film. He had no idea where to start, and didn't care. For starters, he wanted to have a feel of, and kind of sink his feet in Tinseltown.

Another powerful reason to head that way, being closer to his daughter, his only close relative. Last time she'd talked to her, she worked handling the phone and receptioning at a talent agent's office.

Since she'd left Delsol after her high school graduation, they'd only met twice, last time, a year ago. He anxiously wanted to learn how she was doing.

They did keep phone communication. She called up or he would. His idea of a good life for her included a good marriage the old, conservative way. A buddy detective had seen her picture on his desk and had teased him, "How about me for a son in law?"

"It wouldn't be a bad idea," he said, and he brought up the matter over their next phone chat to explore her reaction, "Norma, I think I can get you a nice boyfriend, I know this single guy in the department. He's not too young, kind of shy, but a good worker with a steady job, and he'd love to meet you."

"Please dad, don't insist…" she said, trailing the words.

"I see. You've already got a boyfriend."

"Dad, it's not that… Ah… I might as well tell you now," she added, gathering strength. "I'm gay." And she stopped, waiting for the bomb to detonate. He hung up, flabbergasted.

It took time to digest her last words. He came from initial shock to rationalization. His conservative roots rebelled against the newfound revelation. He never thought her daughter's sex preferences would touch him so personally. He strove to comprehend and do a rapid adjustment.

"Maybe she got traumatized somehow to turn that way. Or, have we, parents, done something wrong? Someone, somewhere done something wrong?" he pondered. "Err…or, there must be an organic explanation."

It didn't take long to accept the new reality. Afraid he'd sounded insensitive, he dialed back and tried one more thing.

"Norma, modern medicine can do marvels. That can be corrected with hormones."

She sounded upset.

"Dad, don't bother. I am what I am, happy as I am. If you don't want me anymore, I'll understand. I'd hate to shame you."

"Don't talk like that. Of course I want you. Always will. Nothing's changed. You're my loving daughter. I'm your loving father. I won't mention it again."

Maravilla's eyelids were about to shut down like lead drapes when he checked into the Gallina Inn. Inside his room, he wet his face with cold water after unloading his luggage, and headed directly for the Gallina Police Department. He asked the secretary-dispatcher for Det Dobbs. This one showed up in the hall and led him into his office.

After the salutations, Maravilla went directly to the pressing matter of the rest stop murders.

"I'd like to volunteer for your hunting posse. I couldn't forgive myself if I didn't," he said.

"There's a $50,000 reward. Active lawmen aren't eligible, but you can collect," Dobbs said, and went on to the meat of the matter.

"According to ballistics, the weapon's most probably a sawed off Remington 870."

"A sure kill."

"We found #4 buckshot casings at the scenes."

"He had murder on his mind," said Maravilla. Dobbs nodded.

"This is the third incident of its kind. A month ago, the stalker wiped out a full family, five people, at the same rest stop. Two weeks ago, he turned his attention to an elderly couple in New Mexico. Same MO: stalk, rob, and shoot the unsuspecting victims in highway rest areas. So far, there are no witnesses, no fingerprints, no car tracks. Incidents took place in dark and foggy mornings, all the targets, luxury cars," Dobbs went on. "Our department is too small to deal with this type of criminal. The FBI's promised to get involved, but they're taking their time."

"Detective, there's no time. Psycho must be caught before he strikes again," said Maravilla.

"Be my guest. Welcome if you wanna get involved. You understand we cannot hire you. You'll be on your own."

"I'm a loner. That's how I like it."

"I'll share the files with you. Public safety's more important. Now, this is strictly confidential. Nothing can leave this office, understand?"

"You can count on that."

Dobbs pulled a file from a drawer and unfolded it over the desk.

"A reporter from The Gallina Gazette who covered a similar crime three years ago found a connection with these three new cases, a rest area murder committed in 20xx. That time, a suspect, Clyde Needles, was caught, tried, convicted, and put to death.

"The first of the new attacks happened the night of December 31, 20xx, exactly the same month and day Needles went to the execution chamber. The reporter called the FBI about the strange parallel. The police issued a point's bulletin for the whereabouts of a Bobby Torino, a Person of Interest…

"He happened to be Needles' companion and lover in the original crime... I'm beginning to think that they executed the wrong guy.

"The files were as thick as a telephone book. The trial offered a wealth of information. From the prosecutor, the defense, the psychologists, and the declaration of the accused themselves, a clearer profile of the criminal duo emerged."

"Know thy enemy is rule number one for victory," muttered Maravilla.

* * *

Bobby and Clyde, Dobbs titled the files:

Clyde Needles came from a well-to-do family in Guaracha Falls, on the Texas-Oklahoma border. His father built luxury houses; his mother was active in church, charities and the PTA. Early on, in his pre-teens, he caught the over-the-counter pill habit. Subsequently, he went into more serious mind-altering drugs.

In constant conflict with parents, relatives and teachers, he decided to hit the road making Mother swear she'd keep the money lifeline open. He headed west and tumbled into Los Angeles, California. He made Mother happy announcing he'd join college to pursue a degree in television broadcasting. Though he never assisted any classes, he successfully milked Financial Aid and his parents out of funds for some time.

Following his dismissal from college, his parents disowned him. He vanished into the urban maze nursing his drug habit with petty crime. He got arrested several times and became a poster icon in the local police precinct.

His life of liquor-and-drug binges continued under the morose nose of parole officers. In his late twenties, he returned home for the last time; but he and his family disagreed practically on everything. Finding finger-pointing and rejection at every quarter, he returned to the city jungle of LA, and the safety found in anonymity.

Junk food and adulterated liquor had changed his appearance. He gained weight. His chiseled, youthful anatomy deteriorated into a caricature of himself ten years later; cheeks, puffy and swollen; once flat stomach, a belly pouch protruding through an oversized shirt; his muscular legs, now hairy cedar logs bumpy with cellulite. The following years he held menial jobs of little consequence complementing his income with small-time drug pushing.

On his 37th birthday he applied for a guard job, the graveyard shift at San Diego Juvenile Hall. His long criminal record didn't show because of a computer blunder. He got hired. They gave him the task of supervising Bobby Torino and forty other problem kids in a section of the Hall.

Serving a short sentence for drug abuse, Bobby's police record was the length of a deprived kid's Santa Claus wish list. Born in a dysfunctional family of an absentee and drunkard father and a mother addicted to dope and boyfriends, he had a sad story to tell. Thin and squalid, acne and meth had ruined his complexion.

Clyde rubbed Bobby the wrong way since their first encounter. Juvie was anything but inmate-friendly. The next day, Clyde forced him into the guardroom and sexually abused him.

The incident was another bead in the rosary of calamities that haunted Bobby since birth. Bobby's screams had no other effect than precipitating laughter among the young inmates of cellblock #4, Bobby's lockup quarters. The abuse lasted several days.

Two months before Bobby's completion of his sentence, Clyde devised a simple plan to help Bobby escape. Wearing civilian clothes, they walked out the door, unnoticed at midday. In the parking lot, they approached Clyde's black Mustang and boarded it. Clyde driving, they slipped away blending with the traffic east.

After a couple hours driving, time came up for a fix. Clyde rolled into a filling station and stopped at the gas pump. He got off and headed in the direction of the convenience store. Bobby stayed behind filling up the tank. Clyde paid for the gas and entered the public restroom. Between walls, he pulled a matchbook, a cellophane bag, and a pipe. He placed two little rocks in the pipe bowl and lit it. He took deep drags. The highs hit fast and he returned to the car. Euphoria was setting in. He slipped into the driver's seat and they got back on the road.

"Oh man, meth: coca, Drano, battery acid, rat poison, and the rest make for an explosive mixture. It feels so good," he said, passing the paraphernalia on to Bobby. "I'm not the kind to let the hungry go hungry. Here Pizza-face, have some."

Bobby had his session with the pipe. He coughed, and soon went into a kind of goofy wooziness to Clyde's delight, who observed him from the corner of his eye.

After a few hours driving the time came to earn some income.

Clyde stopped at River Bend, AZ, a tiny town of ones—one bank, one motel, one eatery, one mini market; all backing up against the railroad tracks. A few old houses and mobile homes littered the arid landscape.

Clyde felt edgy with the pangs of withdrawal. He pulled into a seven-eleven. Bobby looked at him quizzically. Clyde inhaled from the red-hot coals inside the bowl.

"Gotta hit the store," Clyde said. "We're low on dough. Wait here with the motor running."

He checked his service pistol and magazine and put it out of view inside his jacket pocket.

Scarcely five minutes later, Clyde walked out casually, hands in pockets. He scrambled back to his seat. He pulled out a roll of bills of various denominations from under his jacket and flung them to Bobby.

"Count 'em," he said with braggadocio.

He reached to his back pocket and retrieved an Autosport magazine. "Here," he said, "I know you're a car freak."

Clyde gave it more gas. The Mustang re-entered the freeway. They made a clean escape. A few minutes of silence followed. Bobby showed no reaction. *What I've accomplished deserves some praise at least,* thought Clyde. But nothing came out of his companion. Bobby was a strange guy; hardly said a word. Some even took him for a deaf-mute. His attitude sometimes drove Clyde to exasperation.

"I know you don't give a damned shit. Except for that eye twitch that never goes away, you're so fuck'n quiet you might as well be dead, Pizza-face. But I'm gonna tell you how I did it anyway. You might learn som'n."

With mechanical moves, Bobby continued stacking up the bills.

"A slam dunk! The clerk, an Asian guy, turned fuckin' red and puffy when I pushed the piece against his nose. Ha, ha, ha. I ordered him to hit dirt and stay down. Was he scared! Told him to freeze up for an hour, bet he's still down."

The next few hours Clyde kept rocketing eastward along the interstate. He felt a lead-like heaviness shutting down his eyelids. He played with the idea of letting Bobby drive.

No way, Pizza-face's never driven the highways. He's so quiet it's hard to say how smart, or stupid, he really is.

101

Clyde made an exit at the rest area ten miles from the small town of Greyhound, AZ, population 500, still quite a ways from Guaracha Falls, his hometown.

And this is where the versions of what transpired next diverged dramatically. Following is what really happened:

They had to take care of necessities—including a swig of crystal meth. Clyde looked at his watch—three in the morning, the moon, a blotch of dim light, the night, foggy and chilly. Except for his and another car barely visible through the mist, stopped at the rest area across the freeway in the opposite direction, parking lights on, they were alone.

Clyde and Bobby got off, stretched their legs, and walked casually to the restrooms. They noticed the other car's engine idling and smoking out of its muffler pipe. They returned in ten.

The other car had not moved and was still humming. Crawling onto his seat Clyde murmured:

"Noticed the westbound auto parked across the road?"

Bobby nodded.

"That someone inside must've gone to sleep. Why don't you take a look? Ask for donations, you know, cash, credit cards…"

Clyde dug out his semiautomatic from his jacket and put it in Bobby's hand.

"Here, make it snappy. Shoot out a tire. Make sure they don't hound us."

Bobby crossed the road hunching down like a furtive thief. He recognized the brand—a Lexus.

"Not my dream-car, but I wouldn't mind chauffeuring it," he mumbled.

Sliding along the left side of the car, he observed two people sleeping in the front seats.

"Driver must be in his twenties. Mouth agape, he sleeps like an angel in a heavenly dream. Hair's short, crew cut, and he wears glasses… The passenger's a girl, blond, young, good piece of ass…

"They look like mannequins from Sears," he mutters.

Bobby, a southpaw, wraps a handkerchief around his left hand, grabs the gun from his jacket pocket, and taps the window glass awakening the guy. They make eye-to-eye contact.

"You're far out—an alien from another planet," Bobby says appraising his prey…

"Brainy, clean-cut, healthy, well-schooled, the image of success."

His eyes wide and anxious, the man comes out of his dream state into a nightmare that has just begun.

"Buddy, your dreams just turned into a nightmare," Bobby says pointing the gun at his head.

Startled, the young man looks askance at the shiny metal cylinder that reflects the hazy light on and off like an ominous telegraph.

"Open up!" Bobby barks.

A tremulous hand unlocks the door.

The female passenger awakens and freezes. Bobby observes the interior of the vehicle. There are two school duffel bags from the University of California—UCLA—in the back seat.

"Hand over money and credit cards!"

"Quick! The purse. The purse," the young man urges the woman.

"The watch. The rings. The bracelet!" yelps Bobby.

The girl's purse is big enough to hold everything and the man puts the loot in it and hands it over to Bobby.

"Now we're equals," Bobby says as he shoots the man.

The bullet enters neatly under the man's left ear like a knife through butter and exits, not too neatly, out the right temple. It splatters bone and tissue shards over the dash and windshield glass, showering the girl. His cerebrum exploded, the man slumps down lifeless over the steering wheel.

The taste of the girl's companion enters her wide-round eyes and open mouth in the form of blood and brain matter. She comes out of her daze. Her fog-piercing scream reaches Clyde.

"Aaaaah!"

A second shot stabs the mantle of the night. The scream and shot startle Clyde. A prickling sensation crawls up his spine. He circles the car with a clear suspicion of what has just happened but in agonizing state of denial. The slowest seconds in his life. Nonchalantly, counting his paces, Bobby materializes from the fog. Still no traffic either way.

"WHAT HAVE YOU DONE!?"

"Shot 'em dead. Ha, ha, ha," Bobby says through his crooked nose—a relic of one of his father's beatings.

103

Sick, Clyde slouches down and vomits. Two minutes later, he regains a measure of self-control.

"Give me the gun you IDIOT."

Bobby holds the pistol carefully by the trigger ring. Clyde yanks the piece away from him and throws it inside his jacket.

He leans down over the car hood and runs his hand over his head and nape.

"Ah!" he yells, fists banging on the hood. "I told you to shoot down a tire, not them."

"And damage those shiny spoke-chrome alloys? Couldn't do it. Here's the loot."

Grinning, Bobby hands in the purse.

"Oh shit! I should kick your ass," says Clyde recovering from his daze. He hurries inside the car and throws the loot in the back seat.

"Jump on and hold on to your seat. We gotta get the hell outta here before they discover your fuckin' mess. Gonna get off the freeway and take the side roads. We'll get to LA and lay low for a while!"

Clyde u-turns over the median spinning and raising dust waves and heads back west. Once over the blacktop, he flattens the accelerator demanding the most out of the Mustang. The automobile rockets on for a few minutes and leaves the freeway. They arrive at Rosales, AZ, the gas gage needle stuck on the zero mark. Clyde rolls up to the first filling station and buys a tank-full of premium with one of the stolen credit cards.

Minutes later, they're westbound on State-90. They drive without stopping till sunrise. They arrive at Pecos, CA, and pay for a room in a dust-coated motel with another credit card. The clerk hands them the key and waits till they disappear in the hall, then, he dials 911.

"This is Budget Sands Inn in Pecos. A person by the name of Patrick Camello just checked in."

It only takes a few minutes and dozens of lawmen in silenced patrol cars drive up and surround the motel. The clerk leads the way up to the fugitives' room followed by half a dozen cops. Others stay in the lobby or wait outside. Most of them brandish either guns or shotguns. The clerk opens the room with his master key and moves out of the way. The cops storm into the room.

They catch the fugitives spread-eagled in bed. Without meeting resistance, they handcuff and manhandle the suspects out the front door and shove them into patrol cars.

Once in custody, they're read their Mirandas, booked, interrogated and given the paraffin test. The cops soon learn of Bobby's escape from juvenile hall with Clyde's complicity. It doesn't take long, with Bobby's help, to put together the cops' version of the story. Bobby's hands are inconclusive but Clyde's show a trace of gunpowder residue. Clyde's fresh fingerprints appear on the handle of the gun. The murder weapon is his service pistol. The spent casings match his gun.

The pair waves extradition and are taken back to Greyhound, AZ, to await trial. They're two of the most hated inmates in jail.

The people clamor for it and the prosecution asks for the death penalty for both. They're assigned different public defenders and separate trials. Bobby's tried first.

The district attorney offers him a deal convinced he's just another in Clyde's long list of victims, a young impressionable minor falling under the spell of a diabolical psychopath. Bobby reinforces that theory with his own version of the events.

For the culprit, the local newspaper demands the death penalty in its editorial lines. But Bobby is offered a deal, probation after a short time served if he testified against his companion in crime. Authorities consider him an unwilling participant, a hostage. Bobby's testimony agrees with the police theory.

The evidence tends to point to Clyde Needles as the triggerman. Tearful Bobby relates his ordeal since the time of his rape in Juvenile. His image changes from predator to victim. He gains universal sympathy. Public fury is re-focused on Clyde. The cops and the district attorney feel the bile boiling up their throats. Like in the Roman Circus, people clamor for blood.

Bobby's excruciating testimony at the witness stand clinches the case against Clyde Needles. The box of Kleenex travels repeatedly back and forth the jury box. The public defender is fighting against colossal odds.

"The witness account, the forensic evidence, the smoking gun, all point to Clyde as perpetrator of this most heinous and senseless murder of two promising college students, son and daughter of prominent Phoenix, AZ, lawyers," claimed the prosecutor.

Clyde is denied any type of deal. The defender is relegated to fight for a sentence of life without parole as the minor of two evils. Attorney tries to arouse some sympathy for his client by trying the nature versus nurture approach.

"A pill junkie, mind-altering drugs attracted Clyde since an early age. He would pig out on his mother and sister's diet tablets and, like popcorn, on pills from medicine cabinets. He loved the highs for the rest of his life. Drug-induced euphoria kept him awake and restless for days. He continuously lived with hassles and fights in bars and parties and school evictions. Clyde is a born looser."

But not even this rationale and a defense-hired psychologist's testimony that his chronic drug addiction had impaired his mental abilities made a dent in the prosecution's case.

The jury needed scarcely an hour to find him guilty of first-degree murder with especially aggravating circumstances. It took less, a few minutes, to pronounce sentence—death by lethal injection.

Clyde fired his lawyers and refused to file appeals, "They took my past. They took my future. I'll give 'em my balls, but I won't spend my life in a cage," he told his family, who begged him in tears to change his mind. The wheels of justice expedited his sentence.

Three years later, December 31st, 20xx, Clyde walked into the execution chamber accompanied by a pastor. His sobbing mother and sister sat at the witness stands. They observed his demise—society's revenge—at ringside through the plate glass.

One of the executioners pulled the Bible away from his hands. He lay docilely on the gurney and moved his lips in prayer. The society-sanctioned ballet of death continued. The IV needles did their job and Clyde voiced his last breath.

Maravilla rented a new Mercedes and checked out of the motel.

"I don't need this room anymore as I've vowed to touch no hot food or warm bed till I catch up with the stalker—or he catches up with me. Either, or, I don't care," he muttered.

Next three days he traveled aimlessly along the southwest interstates.

"Now I see what retirement age means. Employers know when you can no longer perform at peak. The arrangement I've imposed on myself is strenuous to say the least. I haven't slept in days," he muttered.

The third day on the road, he came down with a bad case of influenza.

He shivered like a leave in the wind with a fever that scorched his temples. He considered suspending temporarily the hunt and checking into a hospital, at least until he recovered.

"Down with pneumonia, how can you be a hunter?" he asked himself.

He took several aspirins and parked at a rest area near a little town in Arizona, but exhaustion finally got the best of him. Folding over the steering wheel, he collapsed into a deep slumber.

In his dream state, he heard shots or firecrackers. Insistent knocking on the driver's window finally awoke him. He opened his eyes and promptly recognized the acned, cyanotic face on the police mug shot eyeing him from the other side of the window glass, the dirty, matted, shoulder-length hair. Bobby Torino pointed a shotgun at him.

Not sure if he was awake or still in dreamland, Maravilla reacted out of reflex. He acted the academy award panic scene in front of his predator. In his feverish state, faking uncontrollable fear was easy task.

"O-okay… d-don't shoot… I'll give you all my money… Everything you want…" he cried.

Maravilla pulled out a Colt 45 semi from his waistband and shot him through the glass between the eyes.

Bobby collapsed like a punctured balloon.

Maravilla got off and touched him. He found no pulse. He grabbed his cell phone and called in asking for two ambulances, one for a dead man and another for a very sick one. His fever worsening, he went into an uncontrollable shiver. He passed out on his seat. He awoke in a hospital bed with Norma by his side. She bent down and embraced him.

"Dad, I love you," she said, eyes wet.

The doctor, the nurse, and Det Dobbs surrounded his bed. Through the open door, a television crew walked in. The many smiling faces gave him confidence. The nurse slid a pillow under his back and he sat up.

"Mr Maravilla, the worst's behind us. You've gotten over it—a particularly virulent strain of influenza," the doctor said, grinning.

"The newspaper wants to take your picture," Norma said.

A photographer snapped several close ups. Surprised, Maravilla squinted. A bearded man in an expensive business suit introduced himself.

"Mr Maravilla, I have an offer from Minerva Studios. They want to put your story to film."

"Really? What a coincidence. I already started writing the script."

They shook hands. They kept snapping photos.

"Mr Maravilla, before I forget, here's the reward money," said Det Dobbs handing him a $50,000 check.

The photographer shot a CU of the check.

───────────